THE ULTIMATE BOOK OF
DRINKING
GAMES

THIS IS A CARLTON BOOK

Copyright © 2006 Carlton Books Limited

This edition published by Carlton Books Limited 2018
20 Mortimer Street
London W1T 3JW

ISBN 978 1 78739 146 8

Illustrations: Peter Liddiard; Sudden Impact Media

Printed in China

10 9 8 7 6 5 4 3 2

DISCLAIMER
Alcohol abuse is dangerous and has serious consequences. The inclusion of a drinking
game in this book should not be considered recommendation for its use. In participating in any drinking games you should think carefully about potential dangers.
   Every effort has been taken to ensure the accuracy and completeness of the informa-
tion given in this book. No liability can be accepted by the author or the publisher for
any loss, injury or damage however caused.

The material in this book was previously published in
The Best Drinking Games Book Ever!

THE ULTIMATE BOOK OF
DRINKING GAMES

EVERYTHING FROM BEER PONG TO RING OF FIRE

Biggie Fries

CARLTON
BOOKS

CONTENTS

Appendix

Introduction

There's nothing that livens up an evening out (or indeed 'in') with friends quicker than a good old-fashioned drinking game. Using the random nature of spinning coins, picked cards, tumbled dice, or the character-based quirks of TV characters, you can quickly turn an innocent night's beer-swilling into a fiercely competitive booze-a-thon where the first stop on your hazy ride is Oblivion Central and nobody is allowed to get off. Together with tongue-twisting word games and more traditional bar-based entertainment, over 100 drinking games (plus numerous variations) have been gathered together in this handy reference guide.

There are games that range from the simple (Beer Mat Catching) to the daunting (Kings) and the terrifying (Drink Don't Think). Games that require skill and strategy (Coin Rugby); games that demand mental agility (Fizz Buzz); and games that necessitate an over-generous chunk of blind luck (see any dice or card game). Everything you could possibly want to know about drinking and drinking games is revealed in this book. You'll be amazed at the number of games you can play with the change in your pocket, or with a pack of cards. And once you've started, you'll find it difficult to stop. The addictiveness of these games is sky-high and when you've found the game that's right for you, it's difficult to have a 'normal' drink again. Open this fascinating little tome and read on...

Important Note: while the drinking games presented in this book are designed to enhance the enjoyment of a night's social drinking, the publishers and the creators of this book would like to point out that, although they do enjoy hearty boozing, they do NOT, in any way, condone drinking and driving. Or for that matter, drinking and cycling, drinking and vandalism, drinking and operating heavy construction machinery, etc. The games in this book are meant to be fun, and a certain degree of planning must take place before embarking on any one of them.

1) Do NOT drive under any circumstances. The very nature of the drinking games here means that you and sobriety will not be friends come the end of the night.

2) Take enough money to be able to buy your share of the drink, and to get yourself a cab home when the hilarity winds up.

3) Carry a pack of cards, a matchbox, some assorted coinage and a set of five six-sided dice – just in case.

4) Stronger drinkers may want to carry a chess set or a small table with them in addition.

• It is illegal to consume beer and alcohol if you are under the age of consent in the state/country/territory you are in. So DON'T do it.

Some Basic Rules
To enable you and your friends to enjoy an argument-free night of heavy drinking, there are a few simple rules that you should bear in mind:

RULE 1: Each game in this book has been carefully categorised and broken down into five separate chunks: the title; the essential supplies that you'll need to play it; the danger factor, which tells you how easy the game is to play; the 'bolloxed factor', which gives you an indication of how drunk you should be before you start to play it; and the main description. A sample layout will look as follows:

NAME OF THE GAME

BRIEF DESCRIPTION

ESSENTIAL SUPPLIES
What you'll need!

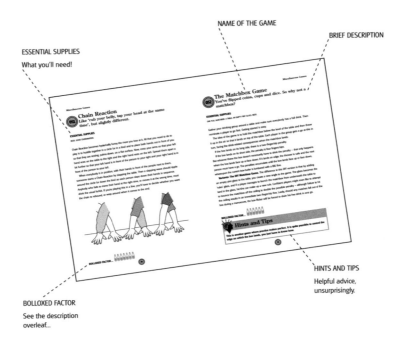

HINTS AND TIPS
Helpful advice, unsurprisingly.

BOLLOXED FACTOR
See the description overleaf...

RULE 2: Beer, lager or cider must be drunk from a pint glass or from the original bottles that the drink came in.

RULE 3: Cocktails or spirits must be drunk from a half-pint glass.

RULE 4: The definition of a pint is eight fingers. One- or two-finger drink penalties can be measured by placing your first two fingers side-by-side on the glass, the first finger at the level of the alcohol remaining. The player must drink enough beer so that the level of the drink drops to below the second finger.

RULE 5: The 'gulp', 'sip' or 'swig' is a bit of a grey area, ranging from a small sip to a big mouthful. Decide which you'll use before you play.

RULE 6: The majority of the games here (unless otherwise specified) are designed to be played with pints of beer. Fines can be halved for those players drinking spirits.

RULE 7: If any player is required to 'down a pint', the drink must be drained completely within 60 seconds.

Additional rules:

- Players are NOT allowed to point.
- Players must drink with their left hand (if right-handed) and vice versa.
- The Thumb Master Rule: One player is elected to be the Thumb Master. At any time during a drinking game, if the Thumb Master places his/her thumb on the table, the other players must do the same when they spot it. The last player to do so loses the Thumb Master challenge and incurs a drinking forfeit — usually a finger/sip of beer. The losing player then becomes the new Thumb Master.
- The Jive Master Rule: One player is elected to be the Jive Master. At any time during a drinking game, if the Jive Master jumps up and 'jives' (i.e. wiggles his/her body around and waves his/her arms erratically) then every player around the table must do the same. Again, the last player to do so loses the Jive Master challenge and incurs a drinking forfeit. The losing player then becomes the new Jive Master.
- The Toilet Master Rule: Sounds disgusting, but it's perfectly innocent. Any player wanting to go to the toilet during the course of a game must ask permission from the Toilet Master. The Bog Lord must then put it to a vote among the other players in the group. If the vote is a 'no', the player cannot ask again for ten minutes. Unfortunate players drink for the required number of seconds. Repeat until people fall over.

Gauging the Gauge

You can gauge how drunk you need to be to play each game by consulting the unique 'Bolloxed Factor', a score out of ten that indicates the perfect degree of confident drunkenness required for playing the game to best effect.

The Bolloxed Factor works like so:

1 OUT OF 10

Booze-free. Somebody asks you to spell 'Nefarious'. You get it right and can suggest some synonyms.

2 OUT OF 10

You've had your first drink. Spelling still isn't a problem.

3 OUT OF 10

Another drink down the hatch. Spelling isn't on your list of priorities right now, but you can spell 'Nefarious' if you have to.

4 OUT OF 10

The world's looking hazy. Somebody asks you to spell 'Nefarious'. You say 'N-I-F-A-I-R-E-U-S' and are quite pleased with yourself.

5 OUT OF 10

The ugly chick at the end of the bar looks remarkably like Angelina Jolie. You could give spelling 'Nefarious' a good shot, but you need the toilet first.

6 OUT OF 10

Pissed. Somebody asks you to spell 'Nefarious'. You say 'N-I- ah f*** it.'

7 OUT OF 10

Wrecked. Somebody asks you to spell 'Nefarious'. You say 'P-I-G'. This is the funniest thing you have ever said.

8 OUT OF 10

Trolleyed. The somebody becomes two somebodies. Both of them ask you to spell 'Nefarious'. You still say 'P-I-G'. When you've stopped laughing they help you up.

9 OUT OF 10

Smashed. The two somebodies ask you to spell 'Nefarious' again. But the enormous pink elephants tell you not to answer the bad people.

10 OUT OF 10

Sozzled. Doctors will later find traces of blood in your alcohol stream. A disembodied voice asks you to spell 'Nefarious'. You can't see or hear anything.

1 CARD GAMES

Card games have been played for fun, for matchsticks and, most notably, for money, but the best way of using a deck of cards is for the wide variety of easy-to-grasp drinking games on the following pages. Making sure you have a pack of cards when you stock up on your beer and spirits will easily spice up a night's raucous alco-quaffing. Enjoy your drinking and don't do anything we haven't already done.

Circle of Death
001 A dangerous game with the prospect of fast, uncomfortably long drinking.

ESSENTIAL SUPPLIES

A PACK OF CARDS. A LARGE TABLE. BEER.

Simple, deadly and effective (but only to be played with cans or pints of beer). Remove the jokers from a pack of playing cards and spread the deck out into a large circle. The dealer then chooses a card from the assembled Circle of Death and reveals it to the other players. The player to the dealer's left picks a second card and also reveals it to the others. If the two cards are of the same suit (i.e. a 2 of hearts and a 7 of hearts), add up the values of the two cards (i.e. 2 and 7 = 9) and the two players who picked the cards must drink for the appropriate number of seconds. If the two cards aren't of the same suit, then the first player places their card on to a discard pile and the third person to the dealer's left draws a card. If it matches the suit of the second player's card, then the values of the two cards are combined and the unfortunate players drink for the required number of seconds. Repeat until people fall over.

BOLLOXED FACTOR...

 Hints and Tips

Try and ensure that people are drinking at a fairly even rate. You can drink a pint or a finger in 20 seconds...

Circles of More Death

002 A deadlier variant of Circle of Death. More circles = more drinking.

ESSENTIAL SUPPLIES

A PACK OF CARDS. AN EVEN LARGER TABLE. YET MORE BEER.

Like Circle of Death, Circles of More Death uses the similar match-the-cards gameplay, but ups the danger and the excitement by having more circles and thus even more chances to drink. Arrange the playing cards in three circles, inside one another. The players sit in a circle on the outside of this deadly card-hoop and the player to the dealer's left draws a card. If the player draws a black card, then he/she must drink for X seconds – where X is the value of the drawn card: 1, 2, 3, 4, 5, 6, 7, 8, 9, 10; Jack = 10, Queen = 10, King = 10, Ace = 11. If the card drawn is red, however, the player can either allocate the whole number to another player, or split it up and condemn two or more players to drink. When the cards in the outer circle have been exhausted, play moves into the first inner circle, where the penalties are doubles (i.e. 1=2; 5=10; etc.) Naturally, when play reaches the third and last circle, the penalties are tripled.

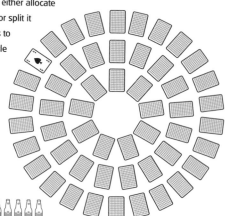

BOLLOXED FACTOR...

Hints and Tips

Try not to get involved in a vendetta early on. It could well cost you dearly in the centre circle.

Cheat
One of the most fun games you can play, given an extra alcoholic edge...

ESSENTIAL SUPPLIES

A PACK OF CARDS. BEER. A SUSPICIOUS NATURE.

Cheat is a game of skill, daring and bare-faced lying. A pack of cards is distributed among the players, who must cheat and scheme to be the first one to get rid of all their cards. Each player will doubtless have some of the same value – two 3s, three Queens and so on. The idea is to lay down these card groups as quickly as possible, whether you have them or not.

For example, in a four-player game, player one might announce that he/she is putting down 'two 6s'. Player two could follow by saying 'one 3'. Player three might chip in with 'two Kings'. In a perfect world, each player would have put down exactly the cards that they said they did. But in Cheat, you don't have to – you just have to make the other players believe that you've laid down those cards. In the example, player one could have lied and laid a 7 and a 3 (either because he/she had two 6s and didn't want to use them, or had no pairs and wanted to get rid of cards quickly). Player two, by laying a single 3, is obviously not lying (but it's a slow way to get rid of cards). Player three could have laid down the cards specified, but could be bluffing.

Shouting 'Cheat', when a player lays what you believe are suspect cards, is the only way to catch them. If they have lied, they must drink a penalty and takes their cards back. If they haven't, the accuser drinks the penalty and gains the cards the last player put down. The game continues until someone gets rid of all their cards.

BOLLOXED FACTOR...

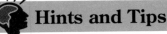 **Hints and Tips**

It's important to show only the top card of the group you're laying down. If you feel extra-sneaky, put down more cards than you say you are.

Ten Brown Bottles

004 Musical Chairs (but obviously without the music and the chairs).

ESSENTIAL SUPPLIES

A PACK OF CARDS. SOME EMPTY BEER BOTTLES (SPECIFICALLY, ONE LESS THAN THE NUMBER OF PLAYERS).

The alcoholic variant of Musical Chairs (without the music and the chairs), Ten Brown Bottles is a game that may end in violence. The idea is a simple one:

The dealer dishes out four cards, face down, to each player (including himself), placing the rest in a neat pile, again face down, in the centre of the table. The empty beer bottles, one less than the number of participants, are also placed in the centre. Now the game can begin. To win, players have to juggle their cards until they have either four of a kind (four Kings, four 3s, etc.) or a sequential 'straight' in the same suit (e.g. 3, 4, 5, 6 of hearts). But changing cards is the tricky bit. The dealer picks a card off the top of the pile (without revealing it to others) and decides whether or not to keep it. Whatever card the dealer chooses to discard, he gives it to the player to his/her left. This player must then choose to discard one of the five cards that they hold, again giving the one that they don't want to the next player. When play reaches the last person before the dealer, the unwanted card gets placed in a new pile next to the pile of cards already on the table. This process continues until one player has either four of a kind or a straight, whereupon he/she makes a grab for a beer bottle. When this happens, the other players must quickly make a play for the other bottles and the loser is the player who is left without a bottle. As usual, the loser must drink an alcohol-related penalty – either a pint, or a large shot of something without a mixer.

BOLLOXED FACTOR...

Hints and Tips

Once you start losing this game it becomes increasingly difficult to play (as your reactions slow), so be alert in the early rounds.

Ring of Fire

005 Perfectly playable and enjoyable – unless you draw the last of the four Kings…

ESSENTIAL SUPPLIES

A PACK OF CARDS. A JUG, BUCKET OR LARGE CUP. BEER.

Put an empty jug, bucket or a large cup in the middle of the table. Deal a deck of cards in a circle around it then, starting to the dealer's left, each person draws a card from the circle. Each card has its own particular consequences:

Ace: ....Everyone drinks one finger/sip from their drinks.

2–5: ......The player who draws the card drinks 2–5 fingers/sips, depending on its value.

6–9: ......The player drawing the card nominates another player to drink from 6–9 fingers/sips, depending on the value of the card.

10: ....The players to the left and right of the person who picks the 10, must drink ten fingers/sips.

Jack: ......The person drawing a Jack must think of a topic, e.g. football, cars, etc., and then each player must think of a type, e.g. Liverpool, Audi. Anyone who hesitates or makes a mistake drinks ten fingers/sips.

Queen: .Grants you temporary safety; do NOT drink for one turn.

King: .....When the first King appears, the player must pour their drink into the container. The same happens when the second and third Kings appear. When the fourth is revealed, the player adds their drink to the jug and then drink its contents. This game takes on a whole new danger if each player has a different drink.

BOLLOXED FACTOR…

 # Hints and Tips

Just DON'T draw the fourth King. When three are down the tension can become unbearable. The Toilet Master has a clear advantage here.

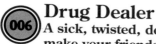

Drug Dealer

006 A sick, twisted, decidedly deadly game that might make your friends hate you.

ESSENTIAL SUPPLIES

A PACK OF CARDS. BEER. MORE THAN SIX PLAYERS.

Separate X cards (where X is the number of players in the game) from the deck and, ensuring that there is one Ace and one King mixed in with them, deal one card to each person. Each player then looks at their card, hiding it from the others in the game. The player holding the Ace becomes the Drug Dealer, while the player holding the King is the Cop. The Drug Dealer then has to wink (slyly) at the other players. Any player who sees the wink must then say: 'The deal is going down.' It is up to the player holding the King, the Cop, to try and work out who the Drug Dealer is. For each wrong guess, the Cop must drink for five seconds. Players can bluff and pretend they saw the wink even if they haven't. But if the cop sees the wink, the Drug Dealer must drink for five seconds and the cards must be re-dealt. This game works best with large groups of people, sat in a large circle or around a table, where the participants can't always see the expressions of the others.

BOLLOXED FACTOR...

 Hints and Tips

Try to avoid playing this in hotels where groups of policemen are staying. Potential embarrassment awaits...

Give or Take

007 **Requires some thought, some maths and the water retention of a camel.**

ESSENTIAL SUPPLIES

A PACK OF CARDS. A TABLE. BEER.

Deal out 36 cards, face down, in a 6 by 6 grid, dividing the remaining 16 cards between the players. The only thing to remember is that the first line of the 6 by 6 grid is a 'Give' row and the drink penalties are from 1–6 fingers counting the cards from left to right. The second line is a 'Take' row and, again, the penalties are from 1–6 fingers. Subsequently, the third row is a 'Give' and the fourth is a 'Take' (on both of these rows the penalties are doubled, i.e. 2, 4, 6, 8, 10, 12). Likewise, the fifth row is 'Give' and the sixth is 'Take' (on both of these rows the penalties are tripled, i.e. 3, 6, 9, 12, 15, 18). To play, the first player flips over the top-left card in the grid and whoever has a card of the same value can 'Give' a one-finger penalty to another player. The second card in the grid then gets turned over by the next player, and whoever has a card of a similar value can dish out a two-finger penalty. When play reaches a 'Take' row, players with a card of the same value as the grid-card revealed must drink the penalty themselves. If nobody has a card that matches the card in the grid, the game moves on to the next one and a higher penalty.

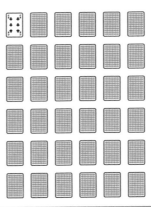

BOLLOXED FACTOR...

Hints and Tips

Remember to keep all players' cards visible to avoid unseemly arguments and possible violence.

Golf

008 Easy. And it has absolutely nothing to do with swinging a club at a small white ball.

ESSENTIAL SUPPLIES

A PACK OF CARDS. BEER.

Deal four cards to each player, face down. Place the remainder of the pack in the centre of the table and flip over the top card. Players can then choose to look at one of their four cards, but can only look at it once. Knowing the value of one of the four cards, the aim of the game is to assemble the lowest possible hand. Each player, in turn, can pick up a card from the top of the pack and exchange it for one of their four cards, hoping that the card they throw away is of greater value than the card they replace it with.

This process continues around the table until someone believes that they have the lowest hand in the game. The confident player shouts 'Golf' and, after the rest of the players get one more chance to improve their own hands, the cards are revealed.

Players then add up the value of their four cards and whoever has the lowest combined total wins the round, by completing the course in the least number, just like golf, y'see? The other players must then drink for a number of seconds equal to the combined value of their cards, calculated using the table below. If the person who calls 'Golf' does NOT have the lowest hand, the value of their hand is doubled and the game still ends. Whoever DOES have the lowest hand is the winner and is spared the need to imbibe. If two or more players tie with the same totals, players must draw single cards out of the deck – the lowest card wins. Card values: Ace = 1, King = 10, Queen = 10, Jack = 10. All other cards are scored at face value.

BOLLOXED FACTOR...

 Hints and Tips

If you're any good at real golf, don't imagine it's going to help you here. It most certainly won't.

Beer Blow
A game of skill, cunning and pursed lips. Gently does it.

009

ESSENTIAL SUPPLIES

A PACK OF CARDS. A BEER BOTTLE.

If the simple games are always the best, then Beer Blow rides high with the greatest drinking games ever invented. Not only is it a chance to embarrass yourself in a multitude of ways (drink yourself into a stupor, blow too soft, blow too hard, and so on), but it also requires a tiny degree of skill and control, something that lessens with each hilarious game. It's ludicrously straightforward: put a pack of cards on top of an empty beer bottle (remember to take the cards out of the pack first – otherwise the game takes longer and it's no fun). Players then take it in turns to blow off at least one card from the precariously balanced pack. Funnily enough, the player who blows the last card or cards off the bottle has to pay the penalty – either two fingers/sips of beer, drinking for five seconds or downing a whole pint. Whatever works best for you.

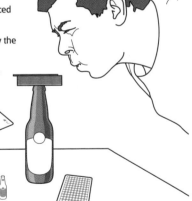

BOLLOXED FACTOR...

Hints and Tips

Make sure you clean your teeth before going out to play this one, it can be a motorway to Halitosis City.

Queens

010 Sentence yourself to the depths of drunkenness with the turn of a card. It's a bit like Snap – but with beer.

ESSENTIAL SUPPLIES

A PACK OF CARDS. MEN. WOMEN. BEER.

Short and sweet but oh-so addictive, Queens is a gender game that knows no boundaries. Shuffle a pack of cards and place the pack in the centre of the table. Each player, starting to the dealer's left, takes a turn and picks up the top card from the pile. If the card is a Jack then all of the male players in the game must drink. If the card is a Queen, all of the female players in the game must drink. Additionally, if the card is a King, all of the players must drink, and if the card drawn is an Ace, members of the opposite sex to the player who drew the card, must drink. There are no penalties for cards 2–10. Unless, of course, you feel that the game is a touch slow for your liking and you want to make some up. Feel free, that's how new drinking games get invented...

BOLLOXED FACTOR...

 Hints and Tips

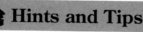

Unscrupulous gentlemen have been known to play the game with two decks and remove a couple of Jacks...

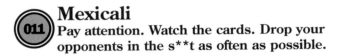

Mexicali
Pay attention. Watch the cards. Drop your opponents in the s**t as often as possible.

ESSENTIAL SUPPLIES

A PACK OF CARDS. BEER (OR TEQUILA FOR THAT AUTHENTIC TOUCH).

Deal out all 52 cards, face down, to the players involved in the game. Starting with the player on the dealer's left, turn over a card. Nothing will happen until player two, perhaps even player three, flips over their cards.

The rules are fairly straightforward and best explained by a quick description of a game. So here's an example of the twisted Mexicali gameplay:

Let's say that player one turns over the 4 of spades. Player two is next up and he reveals the 9 of spades. If he spots that both cards are of the same suit before he plays his own card, player three can then start counting to 13 (4 of spades + 9 of spades = 13) while both players one and two drink for the duration of the count.

When they've finished, player three draws his card: the Ace of clubs. As this card isn't directly related to the previous two in value or suit, nothing happens. But when player four draws the Ace of diamonds, player five can start counting to 28 (Jack = 11, Queen = 12, King = 13, Ace = 14) while player three and four, who both have related Aces worth 14 seconds, drink for the duration of the count.

If player five was then to draw the 10 of diamonds, player six could start counting to 24 (14 for the previous Ace of diamonds + 10) while players four and five drink. Repeat until life makes no sense. If you see snooker on the TV and find it mesmerising, it's probably time to stop.

BOLLOXED FACTOR...

Hints and Tips

Playing this game wearing sombreros is recommended to add that extra Mexican feel. And no one notices when you pass out.

Trapped

012 Imagine the traditional game of 'It' but with cards and beer.

ESSENTIAL SUPPLIES

A PACK OF CARDS. 3–6 PLAYERS. BEER.

Shuffle a pack of cards and divide all 52, face down, between the players. The players are allowed to look at their cards but should keep them hidden from the prying eyes of the others in the group.

Beginning with the person to the left of the dealer, the player can lay down any card he/she wishes; the 8 of hearts, for example. The next player must then lay down a card of the same face value; in this case, another 8. If the player cannot do so, he/she becomes 'trapped' and must drink one finger/sip or whatever penalty is deemed necessary.

The drinker then loses that go and the game passes on to the next player, who can now lay any card that they want. If the player who is currently 'trapped' doesn't have an equal card to match this new card, they remain trapped and drinking.

Play then reverses back to the player on the other side of the trapped player, who lays another new card. If the trapped player still cannot match it with an equal card, he/she drinks again, and the game passes to the player on the other side. This continues until the player is freed and then play continues to move clockwise around the circle until another player finds themselves trapped. When a player has laid his/her last card, the game stops. The other players count up their remaining cards (NOT the value of their cards) and take the required number of drinks. Finally, the winner collects the cards, shuffles and deals again. The game then begins anew.

BOLLOXED FACTOR...

Hints and Tips

This is a good starter game for an evening of alcohol indulgence, as the drinking's fairly steady, but not too heavy.

Poker-head
013 Another beer-drenched version of Russian Roulette. But funnier.

ESSENTIAL SUPPLIES

A PACK OF CARDS. BEER. YOUR HEAD.

Not a game of skill, but literally a game of blind luck, Poker-head takes the bidding basis of the famous card game, and whittles it down to a simplicity that even someone with seven pints of lager, three gin and tonics and a bottle of wine inside them can understand. Simply shuffle the pack and deal one card to each player, face down.

Next, without peeking to see what the card is, each player must pick up their card and place it, with the face visible, on their foreheads. Held there for the duration of the game by a strategically placed finger, the aim of Poker-head is straightforward – whoever has the lowest-value card is the loser. You know what everybody else has because you can see them. But you have no idea what card you have been dealt. Starting to the left of the dealer, each player bets a number of drinks, or fingers/sips if you're playing with pints, that they have the highest card. This continues from player to player until play ends with a bet from the dealer. Players can fold at any time during the bidding, but must drink the current amount of drink previously wagered.

When all bets are placed, the players are allowed to look at their own cards. Whichever player has the lowest card loses, and has to drink the accumulated bet.

Variant: Try playing with more cards. But instead of holding several cards to your forehead, place one there and keep the others in front of you. If using an extra four cards, normal five-card poker rules apply – the loser is the player with the worst hand.

BOLLOXED FACTOR...

 ## Hints and Tips

If your teetotal friends from a freaky religious sect come round unexpectedly, you can just play this for money – they're sure to love it!

Red and Black

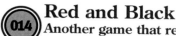

Another game that requires no thought to play. A 50/50 chance whether you drink or not.

ESSENTIAL SUPPLIES

A PACK OF CARDS. A TABLE. BEER.

Place the cards, face down, in a pile in the centre of a table and decide on the number of cards that each player will draw from it (e.g. 10, 15, 20). Simply guess whether the top card will be black or red and then turn it over. If you are correct, nominate another player to drink X fingers/sips (where X is the value of the card drawn). If the guess is incorrect, you must drink the required number of fingers/sips. Picture cards equal 10, and the Ace is high.

BOLLOXED FACTOR...

Hints and Tips

Eat well before you play this game. You may stay quite sober, you may get very drunk indeed.

Suits

015 How slowly can you count? The slower the better in this game.

ESSENTIAL SUPPLIES

A PACK OF CARDS. A TABLE. BEER. SOME FOOLHARDY FRIENDS.

Another simple game guaranteed to set you up on the fast train to Bladderedville. Gather a group of foolhardy players together and sit in a circle. Nominate a player to be the dealer. The dealer calls a suit (diamonds, clubs, spades or hearts) and then deals out the cards, face up, to the players. When a card is dealt that matches the suit nominated by the dealer, the unlucky recipient must drink for the number of seconds shown by the card (picture cards = 10, Ace = 11). The player to the drinker's right must count down the penalty. When the drinker has finished, he/she must choose another suit to continue the game before putting their drink down. If they fail to do this, they receive a further four-second drinking penalty. Simple, but effective.

Variants: Try adding another useful rule – if the player who's counting down the penalty finishes counting before the punished player has finished the beer in their glass, they incur an automatic four-second drinking penalty. As long as somebody else spots it.

BOLLOXED FACTOR...

 Hints and Tips

When you're being forced to drink, keep your mind on the card suit you're going to select next.

Multi

016

A long list of rules. But a long list of hilarious consequences.

ESSENTIAL SUPPLIES

A PACK OF CARDS. BEER. A LARGE GROUP OF UNWARY FRIENDS.

Spread all 52 cards in the pack, face down and in no particular pattern, on a table. The first player then simply flips over one of the cards and faces the consequences. In essence, Multi is a springboard that leaps the game into a variety of other drinking games. Pick your favourites from this book and simply assign them, as below, to the various card types. Players then continue to pick cards until all 52 have been exhausted, whereupon the pack is reassembled, shuffled and spread out haphazardly once more.

Sample actions:

Ace: Everybody drinks.

King: Play Beer Blow.

Queen: Play Categories.

Jack: Play Landmine.

10: Shotgun a beer.

9: Play Thumper.

8: Play Boat Race.

7: Play Beeramid.

6: Make up any rule.

5–2: Drink X fingers (where X is the value of the card).

BOLLOXED FACTOR...

 Hints and Tips

Make sure you've got a full evening ahead of you before you start a game, this may take some time.

Landmine

017

Also known as Asteroids and Drunk Driver.
The name may change, the game is still the same.

ESSENTIAL SUPPLIES

A PACK OF CARDS. A TABLE. BEER.

A simple game for two players. Cut the pack to see who becomes the dealer and who becomes the soldier (highest card wins). The dealer then places six cards, face down, in front of the soldier. The idea is to move from left to right along the line of cards (the minefield), turning each one over and enduring the drink-related consequences. And they are: if the card is numbered 2–10 then nothing happens. The soldier may move on to the next card in the minefield without penalty. If the card is a picture card or an Ace, additional cards are added to the minefield and a mine explodes. The number of cards added is based on the following system: Jack = + one card, Queen = + two cards, King = + three cards, and Ace = + four cards. And to simulate the mine exploding, the soldier must also drink X fingers of beer (where X is the number of cards the player was penalised with, e.g. + three = three fingers of beer). The soldier continues in this manner until (a) he/she is roaring drunk and unable to think or (b) manages to make it to the end of the line of cards. Whereupon another foolhardy Landmine challenger can step up.

BOLLOXED FACTOR...

Hints and Tips

To make the game even more tricky, just add more cards to the initial minefield, but not too many.

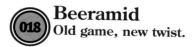

Beeramid
018 Old game, new twist.

ESSENTIAL SUPPLIES

A PACK OF CARDS. PRIOR KNOWLEDGE OF RUDIMENTARY PYRAMID DESIGN. BEER.

Beeramid is an alcoholic variant of the old Pyramid game – the same easy-to-grasp rules, but a greater degree of danger. The dealer lays out 15 cards in a pyramid form (five along the bottom, then four in the next row, etc.) and then gives five cards, face down, to each player. Each card in the Beeramid represents one drink (or if you're playing slowly, one finger). Play starts when the dealer flips over the top card in the Beeramid. Players then look at their cluster of cards and if the revealed Beeramid card is the same number as a card in their hand they can make someone else take a drink. For example, if the flipped card is the 4 of hearts, anyone with the 4 of clubs, spades or diamonds can nominate somebody else to drink. You can also bluff that you have the card, when you haven't, and the other players must then decide whether to believe you and drink or call your bluff. If you call a player's bluff and he DOESN'T have the card, the bluffer must drink double. If you call a player's bluff and he DOES have the card, then you must drink triple. Repeat until blasted.

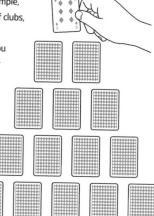

BOLLOXED FACTOR...

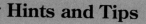

Hints and Tips

Bluffers run the greater risk, but the rewards are higher too. We know what we prefer doing...

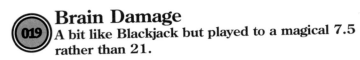

Brain Damage
A bit like Blackjack but played to a magical 7.5 rather than 21.

ESSENTIAL SUPPLIES

A PACK OF CARDS. SPIRITS. SHOT GLASSES.

Grab a pack of playing cards and remove all of the 8s, the 9s and the two red 10s. Brain Damage plays much like the Casino game Blackjack, in that you start with one card and attempt, by being dealt extra cards, to amass a score as close to 7.5 as possible. Picture cards are worth half-a-point (0.5), Aces a point (1.0), 10s are wild, while cards 2–7 retain their face values.

Cut the pack to see which player goes first (highest card wins) – each person in the game must deal at least once. The dealer then takes the pack and, like traditional Blackjack, deals one card face down to the first player and then one to himself. Both players ante up (i.e. bet a drink – spirits in shot glasses tend to work better than beer in this game). The player then looks at the card and gets a chance to ask for extra cards to augment his hand, trying to get as close to the magical 7.5 as possible. If the player goes 'bust' (i.e. goes over 7.5), he/she must drink the bet made.

If the player 'sticks' (i.e. has a hand with a combined total of 7.5 or less), the dealer can then take more cards to try and make his score 7.5 or less. If the dealer busts, he drinks the bet. If both player and dealer stick, extra bets can be made before the two hands are revealed. The loser (whoever has the lowest score) drinks the bet. In the event of a tie, the dealer wins and the player drinks. As in Blackjack, a five-card trick (five cards totalling 7.5 or less) cannot be beaten.

BOLLOXED FACTOR...

 ## Hints and Tips

Having everybody bring along a different kind of spirit adds variety and at least two to the Bolloxed Factor in this game.

Presidents and Arseholes
Initially tricky but easy to master after the first few rounds.

ESSENTIAL SUPPLIES

A PACK OF CARDS. FOUR PLAYERS. ENORMOUS QUANTITIES OF BEER OR SPIRITS.

Deal out all of the cards to the players – this first hand will determine which person gets the title of 'arsehole'. The object of the game is to get rid of all of your cards. Play starts with the person on the left of the dealer, Aces are high, Jokers are wild. Players can throw away any one card, or a combination of two, three or even four cards as long as those multiple cards have the same face value (e.g. two 3s; three 8s; or if you haven't got any multiples, any single card). The next player must then lay down the same amount of cards as the previous player, but they must be of a greater value. For example, if player one puts down two 9s, player two must lay two 10s, Jacks, Queens, Kings, or Aces. If the next player lays down the same card as the previous player, the next player misses a go and must drink (one finger). If the following player can't lay down greater cards, then he/she must drink (one finger). The game ends when all cards have been played, or if nobody can lay any more cards. Now for the twist: the first person out in the opening hand becomes the President, the second the Vice-President, the third an executive and the fourth the proverbial Arsehole. For the following rounds, anyone who ranks higher than you can tell you to drink whenever they want to, but there are some special rules:

The Arsehole must always deal the cards and surrender their two best cards to the President. Conversely, the President gives the two worst cards in their hand to the Arsehole. Play continues until cards become fuzzy and indistinct.

BOLLOXED FACTOR...

 ## Hints and Tips

Avoid playing this game with maiden aunts and visiting clerics. This game is going to get dirty-mouthed in a hurry.

2 MONEY GAMES

Even if you can't lay your hands on a pack of playing cards, all you really need to explore some very fine drinking games is a pocket of loose change and very few inhibitions. Reading through the choice diversions gathered here, you'll be amazed how a pile of coins can be used to enhance the late-night alcohol experience – all of them are drinking games beyond compare.

The One-Coin Game

021 Simple yet deadly. Especially if you play it for more than two hours. And are unlucky.

ESSENTIAL SUPPLIES

A COIN. A TABLE. BEER.

Simple but deadly if played for more than two hours, The One-Coin Game involves gathering a group of friends around a table and nominating an honorary coin-flipper. The game unfolds thus: the designated money-chucker spins the coin into the air, while the player to the left of the flipper has to guess whether it will land on heads or tails. If they manage to get it right, they become the coin-flipper for the player to the left of them. If they get it wrong, they must rush a two-finger/sip fine and are forced to face another 'heads' or 'tails' flip. Only when the player guesses the upturned face of the coin correctly, do the coin-flipping duties move onwards and he/she is saved from further penalty guzzling.

BOLLOXED FACTOR...

 Hints and Tips

Remember to keep a good supply of coins as you'll probably lose quite a few behind benches and down cleavages.

Multiple-Coin Spin

022 The tabletop equivalent of spinning plates on sticks. But without the plates and the sticks.

ESSENTIAL SUPPLIES

A STACK OF COINS. A TABLE. BEER.

A simple game, enhanced by the sneaky addition of increasingly higher alcoholic stakes. Make sure you have a big stack of coinage and a clear table, for the aim of this game is simply this: how many coins can you spin simultaneously on a tabletop? Four? Five? Player one, for example, might bet that he/she can spin three coins at the same time. If successful, the stakes can then be raised higher. But if he/she fails in spinning the number of coins bet, the unfortunate change-spinner has to drink X fingers/sips of beer (where X is the number of coins that the player tried to spin). The betting moves clockwise around the table, anybody unwilling to take the challenge has to drink the current penalty. This goes on until somebody foolishly tries to spin 14 coins at once and is forced to drink 14 fingers/sips of beer as a punishment. How high can you take it? How many coins can YOU spin?

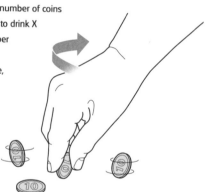

BOLLOXED FACTOR...

Hints and Tips

Practise this at home and see how many you can do. 'A man's gotta know his limitations,' as Clint Eastwood said.

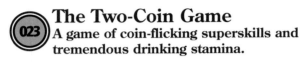

The Two-Coin Game

023 A game of coin-flicking superskills and tremendous drinking stamina.

ESSENTIAL SUPPLIES

TWO IDENTICAL COINS. A MATCHBOX. A TABLE. BEER.

For this easy game to play if you're out in the pub, simply rifle your pockets for two identical coins. Players then gather around a table and take it in turns to flick the two coins from BELOW the level of the table on to the top of the table (fflick the two coins together for a truly random result). When the coins clatter to a standstill, the following rules dictate the consequences:

(1) If one coin lands on 'heads' and the other on 'tails', the coin-fficker suffers no penalty and the matchbox (merely a symbol of whose turn it is, rather than an integral part of the game) is passed on to the next player.

(2) If both land on 'tails', the unfortunate player must down two fingers/sips of beer.

(3) If both land on 'heads', the coin-flicker is allowed to make up an additional rule to spice the game up.

(4) If a coin lands on the floor, the player who flicked them so inexpertly must suffer a four-finger/sip fine.

BOLLOXED FACTOR...

Hints and Tips

Make sure to use any new rule to your advantage. If you're well coordinated, make everyone flip from a metre away, for instance.

38

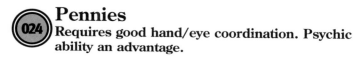

Pennies

024 Requires good hand/eye coordination. Psychic ability an advantage.

ESSENTIAL SUPPLIES

11 COINS (SMALL). A TABLE. BEER.

Known as Dimes in America, the coin game Pennies plays much like a traditional card game (it also works equally as well with distinctively designed beer mats, which may be easier to come by). Best played with five players or less, every player gets a chance to 'deal' the coins. The dealer simply gathers all 11 coins in his/her hand, shakes them about a bit, and then forms a neat little stack, which is then placed on top of the table. Now it's a test of nerve and blind luck – the player to the left of the dealer must guess whether the next coin will be 'heads' or 'tails'. The top coin is then removed – if the player is correct, he/she then moves swiftly on to try and guess the orientation of the next coin. If wrong, the player simply drinks a two-finger/sip fine and continues to the next coin. When the player has worked through all of the remaining coins, drinking or surviving (depending on how lucky they are), the coins then move on to the next player, who becomes the dealer, 'shuffles' the coins and then stacks them up as before.

Variants: More coins equals more chances to drink. Similar to the card-based Landmine game.

BOLLOXED FACTOR...

Hints and Tips

Obviously, anyone clumsy enough to knock the coins over has to drink a penalty. Eleven fingers should be a deterrent.

Spin The Penny

A game of no skill whatsoever. But then they're usually the most effective...

ESSENTIAL SUPPLIES

A COIN. A TABLE. BEER

Another effective, remarkably simple drinking game that's short on rules and big on drunken hilarity. Here's the gist: one player flips a coin, the player to the coin-flipper's immediate left guesses whether it will land on 'heads' or 'tails'. If the player manages to guess the result correctly, then he/she takes the coin from the first flipper and tosses it expertly for the player next to them (and so on around the group). If, however, somebody gets the guess wrong, then the player who chucked the coin spins it on the table and the unlucky player has to drink from his/her glass for as long as the coin keeps spinning. Then, just before it starts to settle, someone quickly smacks the spinning coin down on the table underneath their hand, and asks the bad guesser to plump for 'heads' or 'tails' again. If he/she gets it right this time, the coin is passed on. But if he/she gets it wrong again, the coin is spun yet again and the same drinking penalty applies. Repeat until they get it right.

BOLLOXED FACTOR...

 ## Hints and Tips

Be careful of your glasses when arresting the motion of the spinning coin. A separate table is recommended for the beer.

Anchorman
026 A team game for backstabbing individuals everywhere.

ESSENTIAL SUPPLIES

ONE COIN PER PLAYER. A TABLE (WITH AT LEAST 2 FEET OF CLEARANCE). A LARGE PITCHER OF BEER.

Anchorman is a simple team game that can create a fierce rivalry between opposing teams and players on the same team. At least eight people must take part, or failing that, there must be an even number of potential coin-flickers and drinkers.

Here's how things work: two teams (of equal numbers) sit on opposite sides of a table and take it in turns to try to flick their coins into the jug of beer. Each player only shoots once per turn. When everybody on one team has flicked, the second team tries their luck. This continues until one team manages to get all of its complement of coins into the jug. The losing team then has to drink the jug of beer between them.

But before the losers drink, the winning team must choose someone to be the 'Anchorman' and it's their job to drink last and to finish any remaining beer. Therefore the Anchorman's teammates can be as kind or as nasty as they wish. While drinking, the Anchorman's teammates cannot take their lips off the jug. If they do, they must pass it to the next player. When the jug reaches the Anchorman, he/she has two minutes to drink the rest of the beer. When it's empty, simply refill the legendary Jug-O-Beer and begin anew.

BOLLOXED FACTOR...

 **Hints and Tips**

If you get a draw (0–0 can become common at the end of the night) play again without drinking – you obviously all need to sober up a bit.

Penny Rugby

027 An alcohol-tinged version of an innocent old school game.

ESSENTIAL SUPPLIES

A COIN. A TABLE. BEER. TWO PLAYERS.

A classic, easy game of some skill with a fresh, slightly dangerous beer-related twist, Penny Rugby takes most of the pain out of its more physical namesake and replaces it with liberal doses of liquid anaesthesia.

Here's how it works: the two players sit opposite each other at a table. Using the width of a table, place a suitable coin on the edge so that it hangs half-over the lip of the table. Then, kick off this metal 'ball' by hitting the coin with your flattened palm so that it skids across the table. The idea behind the game is to then nudge the coin with your forefinger so that it skids further across the table and on to the opposite edge. You get three nudges after the initial kick-off, with the ultimate objective being to nudge the coin so it hangs precariously over the other lip of the table.

If after three nudges the coin is (a) still on the table because you haven't nudged it hard enough, or (b) somewhere on the floor because you've nudged it too hard, player two gets to have his/her turn, kicking off as before. If, during your three nudges, you manage to manoeuvre the coin onto the opposite edge of the table, you can then attempt to score. To score a try, reach under the hanging coin with your forefinger and flip it into the air, attempting to catch it with the other hand. If you succeed, you score five points and can go for the conversion. If not, you fumble the ball at the last minute, score nothing and drink a forfeit for your sheer cack-handedness. For the conversion, the opposing player forms a makeshift set

BOLLOXED FACTOR...

Hints and Tips

If you find you drink faster when NOT playing this game, just add some penalties for not getting into a try-scoring position after three nudges.

of goalposts by pressing his/her two forefingers on the table, joining the thumbs together and raising them up like a set of posts. All the conversion-taker has to do is spin the coin on the table and catch it between his/her two thumbs. If caught successfully, the coin can then be flicked (still between the two thumbs) over player two's hand made goalposts. Each time you score, the opposing player drinks. And vice versa.

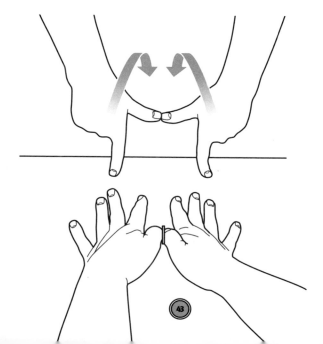

Penny Football

028 An alcohol-tinged version of another innocent old school game.

ESSENTIAL SUPPLIES

THREE COINS (TWO ABOUT TWICE THE SIZE OF THE THRID). A TABLE. BEER. TWO PLAYERS.

Like Penny Rugby, Penny Football involves skidding coins around on a tabletop. Once again, the two players sit opposite each other at a table. Using the width of a table, place the three coins on the edge so that one of the larger coins overhangs the table and the two remaining coins sit in front of it, each one touching the precariously placed coin (the three coins should form an inverted triangle shape). Then, kick off this metallic trio by hitting the overhanging coin with your flattened palm so that the three coins fan out and skid across the table. Meanwhile, the second player closes his fist and extends both the forefinger and the little finger to make a goal (this is then placed on the table, two fingers on top, knuckles of the clenched fist resting against the edge).

The attacking player has to manoeuvre the smaller coin (the ball), by nudging it through the gap between the two larger pieces (the players), into a position where it can be nudged (again this must be through the two larger coins) into the opposing goal. Drink whenever the other player scores against you. The coins eventually pass to the opposing player when (a) a goal has been scored, (b) if the attacking player fails to move the ball through the two players, or (c) if the attacking players shot misses the goal. And no, you can't score with a player.

BOLLOXED FACTOR...

Hints and Tips

If you want to drink more, try giving each player three turns and then having a penalty shoot-out if there's a draw.

Baseball

029 They say that playing sport is good for you. But not this version of Baseball...

ESSENTIAL SUPPLIES

FOUR SHOT GLASSES. BEER. A COIN. SOME MATCHSTICKS. TWO TEAMS OF PEOPLE.

Baseball uses the idea of the popular US sport for shallow, alcoholic ends. In short: four glasses are set up in a row. The nearest is the 'home base', the second is the 'first' and so on. One by one, each player in the team steps up to 'bat', by attempting to flick a coin into a glass. The first glass represents a single dash, the second a double, the third a triple, and the last a home run. Three strikes (if you miss all four glasses) and you're out. Three outs on a team means your innings is over and the other team steps up to bat.

Runs are scored in the same way as baseball. If, for example, a player flicks a coin into the second glass, a matchstick is placed next to it denoting how far that player has 'run'. That player must then drink the contents of every glass up to and including the glass that the coin landed in. The glasses are then refilled and the next player steps up. If that player flicks a coin into the third glass, the matchstick on second base moves to the fourth glass, another one is placed on third, and the player drinks three shots.

If a matchstick passes the last glass, the batting team scores a run and the other team takes a drink. Anyone who strikes out must drink the contents of all four glasses.

BOLLOXED FACTOR...

Hints and Tips

Patience is the key to this game. Aim low and keep the matchsticks moving.

Taps

030 It may sound simple. But Taps requires concentration, focus and good coordination.

ESSENTIAL SUPPLIES

A COIN. A TABLE. SOME BEER.

A simple game with the bare minimum of verbal communication between players, Taps is less a game about shiny bathroom fittings, more a game of skill and dexterity that involves banging a coin on a table.

In this unspoken, fast-paced game, one player starts by tapping his/her coin once. The person sat immediately to the coin-tapper's left then taps his/her coin once and the process continues around the table. Tapping the coin once on the table maintains the current direction of the play. Tapping the coin twice reverses the direction (i.e. from left-to-right, from right-to-left), while tapping the coin quickly three times skips the next player. Play this game as quickly as possible. Anybody who misses a tap, or gets a tap wrong (banging the table when the direction of play has, in fact, been reversed; or tapping without realising that the player next to them has tapped three times, for instance), must drink the usual beer-related penalty.

BOLLOXED FACTOR...

 Hints and Tips

Watch your grandad's antique coffee table when you're playing this one; there'll be marks left.

Spoof

031 The classic coin game. Passport to drunkenness and spoons of lime pickle.

ESSENTIAL SUPPLIES

THREE COINS EACH. A CURRY HOUSE LOCATION. BEER. (OPTIONAL: LIME PICKLE.)

Let's hear it for the traditional curry house party game – a game of skill, of extreme backstabbing, cunning and of large drunkenness coupled with compulsory swallowing of lime pickle. Simply pick your favourite curry location, stock up with beer and make sure that each player has three coins with which to play the game. It works thus: each player puts their hands underneath the table and secretly puts either three, two, one or no coins at all into one hand. This clenched hand is then held over the table and the participating players take it in turns to guess the total number of coins held by all the players (if six people play, that's a maximum of eighteen coins and a minimum of zero). When all of the guesses have been made, the players open their hands to reveal the coins inside. All the coins are totalled up and any player that has guessed the total correctly wins the round and gets to sit out the remainder of the game. With the numbers whittled down a notch, the coin-hiding process begins again. Whichever player is left at the end of the game, having guessed each coin total incorrectly, has to drink a pint in one go and eat a generous spoonful of lime pickle.

BOLLOXED FACTOR...

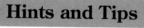

Hints and Tips

You can also play this game in any bar to settle who has to pay to get the next round in. And fetch them. And buy nuts.

Bounce 'Em

032 The quintessential drinking game. Portable. Easy. Deadly.

ESSENTIAL SUPPLIES

A COIN. A CUP/GLASS. A TABLE. BEER.

On the one hand, Bounce 'Em is a game involving skill and luck, not to mention some keen dexterity, a touch of physics and an appreciation of the relationship between velocity and angles. And on the other, it's a game about throwing a coin against a table and bouncing it into a cup. Whichever you prefer.

Gather a group of friends around a table (six players is a good number) and decide who will go first. The aim of Bounce Em is simple and rather obvious – each player attempts to bounce a coin off the table and into a glass or cup of beer. If the coin misses, the next player steps up to try his/her luck. But if it makes it in, the successful bouncer can pick one of the other players to drink a beer forfeit. Shoot successfully three times and you can then make up your own foolhardy rules.

Variants: Bounce 'Em, Drink 'Em: How about this? The glass that you bounce the coin into is also the glass that contains the beer forfeit. The extra element of danger is trying to drink the beer without swallowing the coin that's swishing around in the bottom of the glass. Players who bounce hopeful coins that hit the rim of the glass ('oooh') and narrowly miss going in ('awww'), get another go for free. If a player misses, but he feels confident that he/she will get the coin in 'the next time', the other players can encourage the player to 'chance their arm'. This means that the player is allowed one free attempt and, if the go succeeds the game continues as normal. If the chancy attempt fails, however, the unfortunate coin-shooter must drink all of the beer in the forfeit glass.

Ice Cube Bounce 'Em: In short, instead of a cup, Ice Cube Bounce 'Em makes use of an icecube tray, preferably one with two distinct sides. Play obviously continues as in the original Bounce 'Em game, only this time the coin is aimed at the empty tray. One half of the tray is designated the 'give' side (where drinking forfeits are dished out to the other participating players), while the other is the 'take' side (the shooter must drain the beer themselves, like a L-O-S-E-R). Make it more interesting by shooting your coins from further away each time. Or how about trying to bounce the coins off two tables...?

Speed Bounce 'Em: Said to be more fun than the original game, Speed Bounce 'Em is played at three, four, even five times the pace of your basic Bounce 'Em contest. That means no concentrating, no calculating flight paths, no thinking, no abortive attempts, just simply aim, fire, and miss. If you hesitate, you drink. It's as simple as that.

Bounce 'Em 2: Sit everybody in a circle. Give a coin each to two people sitting opposite each other. Then, quite obviously, each player attempts to bounce their coin into the same glass (this time it's an empty one). The players get as many attempts as they want and, when one of the players does finally get a coin to clink into the glass, the successful person retrieves said coin and passes it on to the person sitting on their left. This process continues until somebody in the circle gets passed a coin when they already have a coin that they're trying to launch into the glass. This person is then mocked mercilessly and forced to drink an entire pint. Very, very quickly.

BOLLOXED FACTOR...

 Hints and Tips

We've found that aiming the coin vertically at the table is the most effective method of getting a decent height on your bounce.

Drop The Penny

033 Think Jenga, Buckaroo, Kerplunk or card pyramids. But with a napkin and a cigarette.

ESSENTIAL SUPPLIES

A CIGARETTE. A GLASS. A PAPER NAPKIN. A COIN. BEER.

Remember the old kids game Jaws? A game where you had to hook plastic debris out of a big shark's mouth before it snapped shut...? Or how about Kerplunk? The old family favourite involving a clear plastic cylinder, straws and a bag of marbles...? Well, Drop The Penny is similar to both of them. Only it involves burning away a napkin with an unhealthy cigarette.

To play, get a paper napkin, place it across a glass and place a light coin on top of it. The aim is a simple one: how much of the napkin can you burn away (taking turns, each player MUST make a discernible hole) without causing the structural integrity of the napkin to fail and the coin to drop? Whoever burns too much of the napkin away, and makes the coin drop into the glass, is announced as the loser and must drink a whole pint of beer as a punishment and get the next round in.

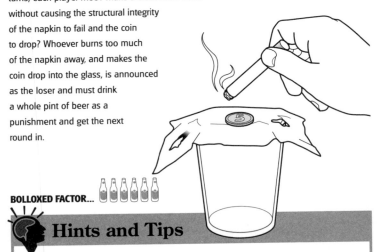

BOLLOXED FACTOR...

Hints and Tips

In the early stages of the game it can be a good idea to burn big holes, speeding the game up considerably.

Chandeliers
034 A game like Bounce 'Em. Nothing to do with ornate lighting fixtures.

ESSENTIAL SUPPLIES

A LARGE GLASS OR JUG. SOME SMALLER GLASSES. A TABLE. BEER.

A bit like Bounce 'Em, Chandeliers moves a lot faster – mainly due to the fact that there are more targets to hit.

Here's how it works: a large glass is topped up with beer and placed in the middle of the table. Smaller glasses (one per player) also filled with alcohol are then positioned around the large glass in front of the other players in the circle.

One by one, the players try to bounce their coins at the glasses. If a coin lands in a small glass, the player sitting nearest the glass must drink the contents and refill it.

If a coin lands in the large glass, all of the players have to drink the booze in the glass next to them. The last player to slam their empty glass down on the table is deemed the 'loser' and must subsequently drink the beer in the pint glass as a penalty.

The glasses are then refilled and the coin passes to the next player. Repeat the game until drowsy. If the room starts spinning, it's probably a good idea to give up. You've gone too far.

BOLLOXED FACTOR...

3 DICE GAMES

The use of dice in a drinking game keeps the competition exciting, as they randomise the dangers and the drinking penalties, creating entertainment where the only thing you can rely on is faith and a large helping of blind luck. We've collected some of the best dice games, ranging from the simple to the more involved, taking in the wildly imaginative and the seemingly stupid along the way. And all you need are a couple of those familiar numbered cubes...

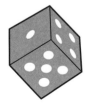

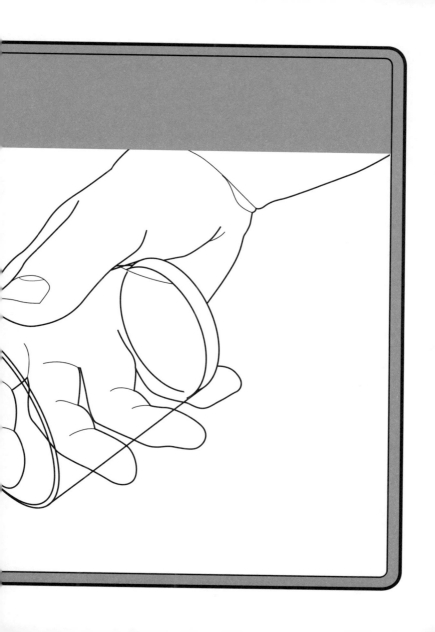

Cheat Dice

035 A slow-starter, but this game is an addictive blend of truth and dare.

ESSENTIAL SUPPLIES

FIVE DICE. A TABLE. BEER. THE ABILITY TO LIE, CHEAT AND SCHEME....

All you have to do is lay your hands on five dice. That'll be enough for you to enjoy this game; an irresistible mix of luck and bare-faced cheek. Like card-based Cheat, the rules are simple.

Player one rolls the five dice (WITHOUT letting anyone see how they land) and, keeping the dice hidden, announces the result. He/she may, of course, 'cheat' by lying. The other players must decide if they believe the player, e.g. whether three 4s, a 2 and a 1 have been thrown or if the roll is actually lower and far less impressive.

If the first player is believed, the next player has a go, aiming to score a higher total (see Scoring) than the previous thrower. Again, the dice should be rolled WITHOUT the others seeing the result and, of course, he/she has the option to 'cheat'. If the total is not higher, the player must drink a forfeit (decided beforehand). However, if another player believes that the thrower is lying about their score, he/she may challenge the total by shouting 'Cheat'. The thrower must then reveal the true roll. If his/her claim is false, the dice-rolling player must drink a forfeit. If the claim is true, the challenging player must drink the forfeit. Play then passes on to the next person.

Scoring: Five of a Kind beats Four of a Kind beats A Full House (i.e. three 4s and two 3s) beats Three of a Kind beats a Pair. Naturally, five 6s beat five 5s, five 4s and so on.

Variant: A more twisted version is Cumulative Cheat Dice, where each player gets one roll more than the previous player to try and beat the last total. That's the good news. The bad news is that the forfeit is multiplied by the number of rolls allowed.

BOLLOXED FACTOR...

Hints and Tips

If you always lose money at Poker, don't try playing this game. Unless, that is, you WANT to get so drunk you can't even fall over properly.

Dice Man

036 Embarking on a Dice Man journey might be the best (and last) thing you ever do...

ESSENTIAL SUPPLIES

ONE DIE. A WILD IMAGINATION. THE WORLD...

Inspired by the cult novel of the same name (in which a man makes all the decisions in his life by simply assigning numbers to the options and rolling a dice), the Dice Man game is not only deadly, but immensely portable, variable and exciting.

The idea behind the game is simple, but highly effective. A player is nominated to be the Dice Man or Woman and the only rule he/she has to observe is that the Dice Man MUST abide by the law of the die. He/she rolls a die, and away you go.

The laws of the die are: the 1 shall always mean that the die is to be immediately passed on to the next player. The 6 shall be an action invented by the thrower (usually an easy one, obviously). The numbers 2, 3, 4 and 5 shall be actions invented by the other players. These actions or tasks can be anything – buy the next round of drinks, chat a girl/guy up in the corner, spill someone's pint and get away with it, steal someone's pint, etc. The only limit is your imagination (tempered by a certain degree of morality and ethics, although don't go too far: 'Tidy up your room' is hardly going to lead to an action-packed night to remember) and a desire to obey the will of the die. So if the action for 3 is catch a train to Glasgow, you should do exactly that. If the die comes to a stop on a 2 (leave the pub and go for a curry) then the die should be obeyed. The actions shall be assigned BEFORE the die is rolled.

Anyone who fails to obey the die, gets a drinking penalty. Let's say a pint. Downed in less than a minute.

BOLLOXED FACTOR...

 Hints and Tips

> **Don't pick actions that are too difficult. The die-chucker will go for a drink forfeit AND remember your unkindness when it's your throw.**

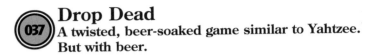

Drop Dead

037 A twisted, beer-soaked game similar to Yahtzee. But with beer.

ESSENTIAL SUPPLIES

FIVE DICE. A TABLE. BEER.

Like Cheat Dice, Drop Dead involves throwing five dice to amass the highest total possible. If there are a lot of you playing, it's a good idea to keep track of the scores on paper.

Each player throws the dice in turn and adds up the total. As long as the numbers 2 and 5 are not part of the roll's total, the player can collect the dice and roll anew, adding the subsequent score (again, unless there is a 2 or a 5 in the roll) to the first score. The player can continue, taking a drink between each roll, until either of the two bogey numbers appear.

If a 2 is thrown then the unfortunate player scores a big fat zero for the roll and the dice that showed the 2 are left out from the next roll.

Likewise, if a player reveals a 5 in his roll, the score doesn't count and the dice that showed the number is also excluded.

For example, if a player throws three 6s, a 3 and a 1 on his first roll, he can boast a total of 22. If on the second roll the dice reveal two 4s, one 3 and two 2s, the player doesn't score any additional points. Having faltered with two 2s, these dice are removed from play and on the next roll only three dice can be used.

Play continues like this, with the player drinking between each dice roll, until a 5 or a 2 is rolled on the last die. When this happens, the player's turn ends, the score is totalled up and the dice pass on to the next player. The winner is the player with the highest total after two rounds of play, and he/she can laugh while the losers drink a suitable forfeit.

BOLLOXED FACTOR...

 Hints and Tips

If you can find a table that adjoins a wall, much fun can be had rolling your dice 'Craps' style, with forfeits for any that fall off.

Three Man

Best summed up as the drinking-game equivalent of 'you're it'.

ESSENTIAL SUPPLIES

TWO DICE. A TABLE. BEER...

Gather a group of players together, and let everybody roll the two dice until someone reveals a 3. When this happens, that player becomes the 'Three Man' and the game can begin.

Each player rolls the two dice in turn, whereupon the gathered players must quickly add up the total and perform the relevant action/task (below). The last person to complete the specified action must drink a forfeit – e.g. two fingers/sips, half-a-pint, etc. If, however, somebody rolls a three (in total) then the Three Man must drink a four-finger/sip or some similar forfeit. As for the tasks, they are as follows:

If the dice show 1 & 3: everyone touches their glass to the edge of the table. The last one to do this incurs the drinking forfeit. If the dice show 1 & 4: everyone puts their thumb on their forehead. Again, the last one to do so incurs the drinking forfeit. If the dice show 1 & 5: a social drink, everyone drains some beer from their glasses. If the dice total 7: the person to the right of the thrower takes a penalty drink. If the dice total 11: the person to the left of the thrower takes a penalty drink. If the dice roll is a double: the dice-flicker adds up the total number of spots on the dice and gives that many penalties away to the group. Apart from the Three Man. If the penalty is given to the Three Man by mistake, then the current dice-roller becomes the new Three Man. If the dice roll off the table: the thrower incurs a drinking penalty for his carelessness. If someone spills their drink: the guilty party incurs a drinking penalty for their lack of coordination.

Note: any dice roll not listed is a 'null' roll, causing the dice to be passed on to the next player.

BOLLOXED FACTOR...

Hints and Tips

Keep a particularly close eye out for the 1 & 3 and the 1 & 4. A little alertness will save you from a lot of grief.

Boxhead
A simple, effective game of chance played with unusual headgear.

039

ESSENTIAL SUPPLIES

TWO DICE. AN EMPTY CARDBOARD BOX. BEER. SPIRITS.

Developed, so it is said, at the University of Victoria in Canada, the Boxhead drinking game is loosely based on the old Three Man game that you should now be familiar with. Like most drinking games, it's easy to pick up, yet the random nature of the game makes it impossible to master. Gather your players around a large table, nominate somebody to go first and then roll the two dice in turn, noting the result and applying the rules listed below.

If the dice total 2: everybody takes a drink (usual penalty of two fingers/sips) If the dice total 3: the person sitting to the left of the dice-roller drinks. If the dice total 4: nothing happens; move on to the next player. If the dice total 5: roll another die. The result equals the number of fingers/sips everyone at the table must drink. If the dice total 6: the dice-roller can make up a new rule. Further rolls of 6 will activate this new rule, although the dice-roller can make up a new one afterwards if he/she wishes. If the dice total 7: players slap their hands down on the table. The last one to do this drinks. If the dice total 8: roll another die. The result equals the number of fingers/sips that are poured into a glass for the dice-roller to drink. If the dice total 9: the person sitting to the right of the dice-roller drinks. If the dice total 10: toilet break. Unless you can roll a 10 you won't be allowed to leave the table. If the dice total 11 or 12: Boxhead! The dice-roller must wear the cardboard box on their head (this is particularly effective in pubs) until he/she rolls another 11 or 12 to remove it. However, if another player rolls an 11 or 12, the box is automatically transferred to them. And, worse than the indignity of wearing a box on your noggin, the Boxhead must also drink whenever anybody else in the game drinks. With some difficulty, obviously.

Variations: Double Boxhead: Double Boxhead follows Boxhead rules, the only real difference being that there are two boxes in play. So, the first player to roll an 11 or 12 wears one box, the second player to do so gets the other one. The same rules apply to get rid of the box. Players cannot wear two boxes (unless the boxes are different sizes and it is funny).

Triple Death Boxhead: Like Boxhead, but with THREE dice instead of two... This game dares you to carry out all possible combinations of the three dice rolled, following the original game's rules. For example, if a 3, a 6 and a 2 are rolled, all of the following actions apply: 3 + 6 = 9 (the person sitting to the right of the thrower drinks); 3 + 2 = 5 (roll another die. The result equals the number of fingers/sips everyone must drink); 6 + 2 = 8 (roll another die. The result equals the number of fingers/sips that are poured into a glass for the thrower to drink). Three times the fun...

Pinball Boxhead: Whenever a player finishes a drink, they should place the empty glass/can in front of them on the table. Eventually, each player should have built up a wall of empties. The dice are then rolled one at a time, with the aim being to bounce the dice off the other players' walls. If you bounce them off two walls, double the eventual penalty. Off three walls, then triple it. When both dice have landed, the usual Boxhead rules apply, modified by the pinball bonus. If the dice should leave the table during a throw, the dice-roller must finish his beer in one go.

BOLLOXED FACTOR...

 Hints and Tips

On no account hit the cardboard box while it is on someone's head. They won't know who's doing it and may become agitated.

Magic Dice

040 Another random drink-a-thon, and perfect for loudmouths everywhere.

ESSENTIAL SUPPLIES

ONE DIE PER PLAYER. A TABLE. BEER.

Before every round of Magic Dice, pick a player to be the 'mouth' and then give everybody in the group one die. The rules are simple – in a fit of choreographed recklessness, all of the players roll their dice on to the table simultaneously. At the same time, the designated 'mouth' calls out a number between 1 and 6 and the players incur a forfeit (the usual two-fingers/sips will suffice) if the number yelled matches the spots shown on their tumbled dice. The 'mouth' can also mix things up a bit by calling either 'even' or 'odd', whereupon anybody who has an even or odd number on his/her die, incurs double the usual penalty. There's an added risk, however, because if the 'mouth' calls even and ends up with a 2, 4 or 6 showing on his/her own die, or calls odd and is unfortunate enough to get a 1, 3 or 5, he/she must drink triple the two-finger/sip penalty.

BOLLOXED FACTOR...

Hints and Tips

To avoid any possible die confusion, try to have a different coloured die for each person (and make sure they remember which is which).

Threshold

041 Heads or tails? Guess the orientation of the coin or pay the liquid penalty.

ESSENTIAL SUPPLIES

A DIE. A CUP. A COIN. A TABLE. BEER.

How simple can a game be? Even after seven pints of lager, a couple of gins and a curry, the rules for this game remain crystal clear and addictively simple. (1) Get a cup. (2) Put the die and the coin in the cup. (3) Each player gets a chance to shake the contents of the cup and to ask the player next to them to guess whether the coin will land on 'heads' or 'tails'. (4) The shaker of the cup then empties the die and the coin hopefully on to the tabletop, noting the orientation of the coin and the number shown on the die. (5) If the guessing player gets the 'heads'/'tails' forecast correct, the shaker of the cup is forced to drink X fingers/sips of beer – where X is the number shown on the die. (6) If the guessing player gets the 'heads'/'tails' forecast wrong, however, he/she must drink as many fingers/ sips at the upturned die has spots.

Variations: Stupid Threshold: Essentially the same as Threshold, but played with two coins.

Bloody Stupid Threshold: Essentially the same as Stupid Threshold, but played with two coins and two dice.

BOLLOXED FACTOR...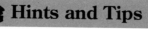

Hints and Tips

To avoid confusing yourself, write 'heads' or 'tails' clearly on a beer mat in front of you and shout it when someone asks.

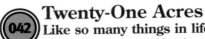

Twenty-One Acres

042 Like so many things in life, this one's simple to learn, but very difficult to give up.

ESSENTIAL SUPPLIES

FIVE DICE. BEER. SPIRITS.

Another tiny but effective game that's easy on a beer-addled brain and a breeze to learn. Unlike other dice games, which count all of the numbers on a die, Twenty-One Acres is only interested in the amount of 1s that are rolled by the participating players.

Here's how it works: each player takes it in turn to roll the five dice. If a 1 is rolled then the players either make a mental note of it or scribble it down on a handy piece of paper, beer mat or cigarette packet. The player that rolls the seventh 1 of the game is the player who gets to pick what drink will be consumed later in the game (beer, vodka, gin, whatever your poison). The player who rolls the 14th 1 of the game is the player who gets to pay for the drink specified earlier. Finally the player who rolls the 21st 1 is the lucky soul who gets to drink the chosen (and now paid-for) drink in one.

BOLLOXED FACTOR...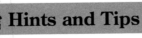

Hints and Tips

It's wise to limit the size of the drink that's picked, to avoid the evening becoming uncontrollably expensive.

Bunko
(043) A game for the early evening, when players can still string thoughts together.

ESSENTIAL SUPPLIES

SIX DICE. TWO TABLES. EIGHT PLAYERS. BEER. SOME PAPER. A PEN.

Bunko is a slightly complex dice game that's played in rounds and can only be played with groups of four people. The aim is for your team (two players) to amass 21 points before the opposing team (two players) does.

If there are eight players (two teams of four), these are split between two tables – two play two on table 1 and two play two on table 2. Team partners sit opposite each other and, rolling three dice in turn, each player tries to get as many 6s as possible. Each 6 rolled is worth one point, and the player in control of the dice keeps rolling until none of the three dice shows a six. When this happens, play passes to the next player on the opposing team, and so on around the table. The winners are the first partnership to make it to the magical 21-point total with their combined scores.

However, there are certain rules. Firstly, if a player rolls three 1s, the team loses all their points in a 'wipeout'. If a player rolls three 6s, the 'Bunko', the rolling player gets three points, while both teams get the chance to earn a bonus. Whenever a Bunko appears, anyone, from either team, can try to pick up the dice. Each die recovered is worth an extra point. Winning partnerships then swap tables, playing the other team members.

And where exactly does the excessive drinking come in? 'Wipeouts' could be punished with a drinking forfeit; Bunko rolls could penalise the rolling team if they don't retrieve at least two of the three dice up for grabs. You can also make up penalties for if a team rolls three 2s, 3s, 4s or 5s. The possibilities are endless. Why not try a couple of games for yourself?

BOLLOXED FACTOR...

 Hints and Tips

> You have to be poised to be quick off the mark when a 'Bunko' occurs. This should be the responsibility of the non-dice-thrower.

Dice Games

Six Pack
044 A fast-paced game of glass-filling and glass-emptying.

ESSENTIAL SUPPLIES

A DIE. SIX GLASSES. BEER.

Arrange six glasses (half-pint tumblers for amateurs, pint-glasses for the pros) in a row and number them from 1–6. Half-fill glasses 1, 3 and 5 with beer and leave the others empty. Now take your trusty die, pick somebody to go first and begin as follows:

Each player rolls the die and, on seeing the result, picks up the corresponding glass. If it's a full glass, then the player drinks the beer and then passes the die on to the person to his/her left. If it's an empty glass, the player is obliged to pour some of his own drink into it, before passing the die on to the next player. This process continues around the table until people are either (a) drunk, or (b) annoyed that they've given away too much beer. Drunkenness or penniless sobriety rests on the throw of the die...

BOLLOXED FACTOR...

Hints and Tips

This is a game that becomes much more fun if everybody's drinking something different. Variety is the spice, etc.

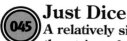

Just Dice

045 A relatively simple game. As long as you jot down the string of penalty rules.

ESSENTIAL SUPPLIES

TWO DICE. BEER. SPIRITS.

Similar to Three Man, Just Dice is a much simpler, quicker game, but still one that gets you sloshed out of your brain in under two hours. The rules are straightforward – each player rolls two dice and notes the numbers that come up. Rolls that add up to a 6 (1 & 5, 2 & 4) or have a 6 in them (6 & 1, 6 & 2, 6 & 3, 6 & 4, 6 & 5), incur the traditional beer-down-the-hatch penalty. In addition, rolling a double 2, double 4 or a double 5 incurs an X finger/sip penalty (where X is the number of the double thrown). A double 3 incurs two separate penalties, the usual two-finger/sip penalty for having two numbers that add up to 6, plus a three-finger/sip penalty for the double. Worse still, roll a double 1 or a double 6 and the player to your left gets to pour you a shot of your least favourite spirit. You, naturally, must down it in one.

BOLLOXED FACTOR...

 Hints and Tips

When asked what your least favourite spirit is, you **MUST** tell the truth. To do otherwise would be unprincipled. Ahem.

Mexican
046 A slightly more complicated than ususal game of Mexicans, Scumbags and point-scoring.

ESSENTIAL SUPPLIES

TWO DICE. A PEN. SOME PAPER. BEER.

Slightly more involved than most drinking games, Mexican can nevertheless lead to a long and competitive evening of drunkenness. Again, like Three Man and Boxhead, the game involves rolling two dice and performing the tasks (drink-related, of course) that are associated with them. In this case, however, Mexican is also about amassing a decent score over your opponents. Dice rolls are subject to the following punishments and penalties:

If the dice show 1 & 2: this is called a 'Mexican', the lowest possible roll and so the most nasty. Every time a Mexican is thrown, the standard drink penalty (let's say, one finger/sip of beer) is doubled. If the dice show 1 & 3: this is known as a 'Scumbag'. The dice-roller must immediately finish his current drink, whether it's a quick shot of Tequila or a full pint of lager. If the dice show a double: the dice-thrower's score increases by the number of the double multiplied by 100 – i.e. if a double 2 is thrown, the player's score increases by 2 x 100 = 200. Any other throw: another scoring roll. Simply take the highest number on the two dice and multiply it by 10 + the smallest number – i.e. 6 & 4 scores 64, 3 & 2 scores 32.

The player that starts the game has a choice of taking up to three rolls to get the highest score possible. However many you decide to take, the final score is always the total amassed on the last throw, whether it's the first, second or third attempt. Once the starting player has decided on how many dice rolls he/she is going to make, the other players must follow suit. For example, if the starting player decides to take only one dice roll, everybody else in the game can only take one roll too. However, the two dice do NOT have to be thrown at the same time. If a player has more than one throw available, he/she can elect to only roll one of the two dice the second time around. Therefore, if a player has two throws available, and rolls a 5 & 1 on the first go, he/she may decide to only pick up the 5 and to throw that die again (thereby increasing the chances of a Mexican or a Scumbag). But, as the object of the game is to amass the highest score, the player may want to rethrow the 1 to increase the points total. The loser is the player who scores the lowest and so he/she must incur the penalty drink as a result.

Variant: Mega-Mexican: For real masochism, try adding a third die; one that's a different colour to the two point-scoring dice. Thus, when drinking penalties occur, the player must not only drink the traditional finger/sip punishment (and this may have been increased by Mexicans during the game), but he/she must repeat the penalty X times (where X is the number on the third die).

BOLLOXED FACTOR...

Hints and Tips

As this game goes on, try to keep track of the scores carefully. Some of your fellow players will get 'forgetful' or 'numerically challenged' after a couple of rounds.

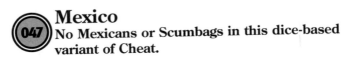

Mexico
047 No Mexicans or Scumbags in this dice-based variant of Cheat.

ESSENTIAL SUPPLIES

TWO DICE. A CUP. A PEN. SOME PAPER. BEER.

As another version of the Mexican game, Mexico not only refines the rules, but makes the gameplay slightly more dangerous by introducing an element of bluff.

Again, Mexico revolves around the chucking of two dice on to a table, but this time the dice are rattled around in a cup that is slammed down to hide the dice roll from the others. The thrower is allowed to look at the result and the highest number is multiplied by 10 and added to the lower number. Rolling a 5 and a 6, for example, would give a score of 65. But, as you have to roll a better score than the previous player, you may have to lie about it. Dice rolls are ranked in the following order: 1 & 1; 2 & 1; other doubles (6 & 6, 5 & 5, etc.); 6 & 5; 6 & 4; 6 & 3; 6 & 2; 6 & 1 and so on.

Once the dice-roller has announced his score, he waits for somebody to challenge him. If nobody does, the dice move on to the next player. If, however, the dice-roller IS challenged, the challenger can lift the cup to see if the dice-roller is telling the truth. If he/she was, the challenger must drink half-a-pint of beer. If the dice-roller is proved to be a liar, he/she downs the half.

Special rules apply for rolls of 1 & 1 (tell any opponent to drink half-a-pint... if they don't believe you but you have rolled a true 1 & 1, this penalty is doubled) and rolls of 1 & 2 (which changes the direction in which the dice are passed around the table).

Extra rules: if you drop a die (and someone notices), drink one finger/sip. If you drop both dice, drink two fingers/sips. If you slam the cup down on the table and one die sneaks out, drink one finger/sip. If you lose a die, drink a whole pint.

BOLLOXED FACTOR...

 ## Hints and Tips

Make sure you understand the ranking system of the different rolls before you start bluffing, otherwise you'll definitely come a cropper.

Speed Dice

048 Roll the dice, drink the beer. What could be simpler?

ESSENTIAL SUPPLIES

TWO DICE. BEER.

Short and sweet, all you need for a passport to oblivion is a pair of dice and a table to chuck them on to. Everybody in the group rolls two dice and adds up their score. The loser is the player with the lowest combined score from the two dice and must drink the difference between the highest score and the lowest score in fingers/sips. If there is a tie for the lowest score, both losers must drink the hefty forfeit.

Variant: If any player rolls a 6, they get to roll that die again adding the extra number to the total. Larger totals = bigger differences. And ultimately this means more drinking.

BOLLOXED FACTOR...

Hints and Tips

The only advice we can offer when playing this game is to wear a helmet. It'll help when you fall over.

Forfeit Dice

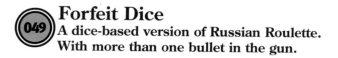

049 A dice-based version of Russian Roulette. With more than one bullet in the gun.

ESSENTIAL SUPPLIES

THREE DICE. A TABLE. BEER.

Before play starts, take some time out to decide on six individual forfeits (e.g. drinking two fingers/sips of beer, downing your pint, buying the next round, etc.) and to assign each one a number from 1–6. Set one of the three dice aside – this will be known as the 'forfeit die' and will be used to decide which one of the six penalties you have created will be applied to losing players. Now for the game itself – each player in turn takes the two remaining dice and rolls them in full view of the other players. The next player must then guess whether his dice-roll will have a higher total than the previous players. When he/she has plumped for 'higher' or 'lower', the dice are rolled and result examined. If the player is right, then he/she gets to roll the dice for a second time, again guessing whether the total will be 'higher' or 'lower' than the first. If the player is correct again, then play passes on to the next player in the group. Two correct guesses in a row and play passes on to the next player in the group. If, however, a dice-rolling player gets two guesses wrong back-to-back, then he/she must pay a forfeit, which is decided randomly by rolling the 'forfeit die'.

BOLLOXED FACTOR...

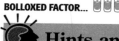

Hints and Tips

Students of odds will tell you that a 7 is the most common total with two dice. That may help you.

7-11-Doubles

(050) A fast-paced game with lots of booze that requires a minimum of brainpower.

ESSENTIAL SUPPLIES

TWO DICE. A TABLE. AN EMPTY PINT GLASS. BEER.

Another simple dice game, laced with the possibility of extreme drunkenness. Each player takes two dice and rolls them, taking careful note of the result. If the dice-chucker comes up with a 7, an 11, or any double, then he can pick somebody at random to drink a forfeit.

The forfeit: whoever is chosen must first locate the empty pint glass (making sure NOT to touch it with their hands) and then fill it half-full with beer.

The aim of the game is for the forfeiting player to drink the contents of the pint glass BEFORE the player with the dice manages to roll another 7, 11 or double. The player with the dice cannot roll them until the forfeiting player has touched the pint glass.

If the forfeiting player manages to drink the beer in the glass before the dice show any of the relevant bogey numbers, then play passes on to the next player. If, however, the forfeiting player does not manage to drain the amount of penalty booze before a 7, 11 or double is rolled, then another half of beer is added to the glass and the process begins again. This continues until the player beats the dice-roller.

Note: any form of abuse of the dice by anybody in the game – throwing them wildly off the table, clattering them into other people's drinks, seeing if you can bounce them down the corridor and through the toilet doors – incurs a hefty one-pint penalty.

Also note: if the penalty beer glass is ever filled, a fresh glass shall be sought out and the excess penalty deposited therein.

BOLLOXED FACTOR...

Hints and Tips

If you have to pay the forfeit, make sure you've got everything planned BEFORE you touch the pint glass. Or suffer the consequences.

4 MISCELLANEOUS GAMES

They're the games that don't seem to fit in anywhere else. Games that don't need dice, cash, a TV or cards, just an open mind and rock-hard drinking stamina. What they might need, however, are things like matchboxes, beer mats, empty bottles, pool tables or dart boards. They're easy to pick up, addictive to play and immensely satisfying (as long as you're not the dribbling, hazy-headed loser at the end of the evening).

Chain Reaction

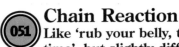

051 Like 'rub your belly, tap your head at the same time', but slightly different.

ESSENTIAL SUPPLIES

BEER. GOOD COORDINATION.

Chain Reaction becomes hysterically funny the more you lose at it. All that you need to do to play is to huddle together in a circle (or in a line) and to place both hands out in front of you so that they are resting, palms down, on a flat surface. Now, cross your arms so that your left hand rests on the table to the right and the right hand rests on the left. Spread them apart a bit further so that your left hand is in front of the person to your right and your right hand is in front of the person to your left.

When everybody is in position, with their hands in front of the people next to them, someone starts a Chain Reaction by slapping the table. Then a slapping wave should ripple around the circle (or down the line) as each person slaps down their hands in sequence. Anybody who fails to move their hand at the right time, or moves it at the wrong time, must drink the usual forfeit. If you're playing this in a line, you'll have to decide whether you want the chain to rebound, or wrap around when it comes to the end.

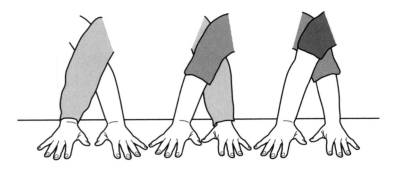

BOLLOXED FACTOR...

The Matchbox Game

052 You've flipped coins, cups and dice. So why not a matchbox?

ESSENTIAL SUPPLIES

ONE FULL MATCHBOX. A TABLE. AN EMPTY PINT GLASS. BEER.

Gather your drinking group around a table and make sure everybody has a full drink. Then nominate a player to go first. Getting started is easy.

The idea of the game is to hold the matchbox below the level of the table and then throw it up in the air so that it lands on top of the table. Each player in the group gets a go at this in turn, facing the drink-related consequences when the matchbox lands:

If the box lands on its long side, there is a two-finger/sip penalty.

If the box lands on its short side, the penalty is four fingers/sips.

But whoever threw the box doesn't necessarily have to drink the penalty – that only happens when the box lands face up or face down. If it lands on edge, the thrower is safe and the next person must have a go. The penalties accumulate until the box lands face up or face down, whereupon the current box-hurler is lumbered with a BIG fine.

Variants: The DIY Matchbox Game. The difference in this DIY version is that by adding an empty pint glass to the table, you create a new angle to the game. The glass becomes the 'rules' glass, and if a player manages to launch the matchbox from underneath the table to land in the glass, he/she can make up a new rule. Confident players might even like to attempt to bounce the matchbox off the ceiling to double the possible penalty – although failure to hit the ceiling results in an immediate two-finger/sip fine. Lastly, should any matches fall out of the box during a manoeuvre, the box-flicker will be forced to drain his/her drink in one go.

BOLLOXED FACTOR...

 Hints and Tips

This is another game where practice makes perfect. It is quite possible to control the edge on which the box lands, you just have to know how.

Timber!
053 A version of the old favourite Jenga – but on the cheap and with beeer.

ESSENTIAL SUPPLIES

AN EMPTY BOTTLE. A FULL MATCHBOX. BEER.

Like building a stack of playing cards, Timber! offers a similar challenge to the thrill-seeking drink junkie, but one that takes its design and inspiration from the familiar pub environment.

It is simply this: players place an empty beer bottle in the middle of the table and then attempt to stack as many matches as they can on the neck. With full drinks in front of each player, participants take it in turn to add another match to the precariously balanced, ever-growing pile of wood on top of the bottle. The loser is the one who successfully adds his/her match, but in doing so, knocks the rest on to the table. When this happens, all players are duty-bound to shout 'Timber!' and to mock the player who ended the game. If mocking is not sufficient, however, the penalty should be to down a drink in under 30 seconds. Or 20, if you're feeling a little harsh...

BOLLOXED FACTOR...

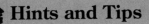 **Hints and Tips**

A slightly sneaky thing to know is that a little moisture can help the matchsticks stick together...

Beer Pong

Another game that involves flicking an object into other people's drinks.

ESSENTIAL SUPPLIES

SOME GLASSES OF BEER. A PING-PONG BALL. A TABLE.

Judging by the title and the 'essential supplies', you're probably thinking that Beer Pong is just another 'flick-an-object-into-an-opponent's-beer' game. Well, you're absolutely right. Trying to get everyday objects into other people's drinks (preferably by launching them into the air) forms the backbone of many a classic drinking game and Beer Pong is not one to shirk hundreds of years of tradition.

Best played with either two players or two teams of two, participants should arrange the glasses of beer like a wall in front of them – four to six glasses ought to be sufficient. Then, yes, each player or team takes it in turn to try and get the ping-pong ball into the opposing team's glasses. Naturally, if a ball does land in a cup, then the opposing team is forced to drink the contents. The empty glass is then taken out of the line, leaving only the full/half-full glasses in play. Repeat until drunk. The first team or player to land a ping-pong ball in all of the opposing team's glasses is the winner.

BOLLOXED FACTOR...

 Hints and Tips

Ping-pong balls are very light. The occasional judicious sneeze or sneaky blow might be enough to knock it off course...

The Pool Drinking Game
An enticing mix of two great pub traditions – beer and pool.

ESSENTIAL SUPPLIES

A POOL TABLE. CUES. BALLS. BEER.

Play a game of pool as normal, but add these simple penalties and forfeits to spice up the green-baize action. (1) For every shot that doesn't pot a ball – excluding foul balls – drink one finger/sip from your pint. (2) Foul shots – missing your ball, hitting an opponent's ball, moving a ball with your hand, etc. – drink two fingers/sips. (3) Potting the white ball, drink four fingers/sips. (4) Potting the black ball – when you're not supposed to – drink a hefty eight fingers/sips. Theoretically, the more you drink, the worse you play. And the worse you play, the more you are forced to drink. A vicious circle...

Variants: Killer: Rack up the pool balls as normal. But this time, players MUST pot a ball (of any colour, except the white) whenever they visit the table. Each player gets one shot (except the player who breaks off, he/she is allowed two shots to pot a ball).

If a player pots a ball, he/she then leaves the table and lets the next player on. If a player fails to pot a ball during a visit to the table, he/she loses one of three lives and incurs a two-finger/sip fine. The player with the most lives left at the end of the game, wins.

Drink The Difference: Play a game of pool as normal. But for every ball that is left on the table after the winning player has potted the black, the loser must drink a two-finger/sip penalty.

BOLLOXED FACTOR...

 Hints and Tips

Try and avoid playing this with anyone who says that they've "played the odd game of pool" – you're probably gonna get beat.

Mouth-Lift Truck

056 A game that requires a strong set of teeth or astonishing oral suction.

ESSENTIAL SUPPLIES

AN EMPTY BOTTLE. BEER.

A silly, throwaway game, designed to embarrass anyone who's perky enough to say 'Yeah, ok. I'll do it.' Simply place an empty bottle on the floor and challenge the players to pick it up with their mouth. Of course, it's a bit more difficult than just getting down on all fours, leaning over and picking the bottle up between your teeth. To make things difficult, players must first stand on one leg, holding their other leg behind their body with their right hand. Not only that, but to keep the left hand busy, it must continually keep hold of the right ear throughout the bottle-grabbing manoeuvre. Lift the bottle off the floor to avoid drinking a two-finger/sip fine. But even if you fail, it's worth it just to see how many people fall flat on their faces, or how human balance is disrupted by the presence of eight pints of lager...

BOLLOXED FACTOR...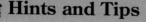

 **Hints and Tips**

Try and go first. Once that beer bottle's had everybody's lips around it, it's going to be well slippy...

Beer Roulette

057 An alluring mix of Russian Roulette and shotgun can-drinking.

ESSENTIAL SUPPLIES

A SIX-PACK OF BEER.

The frightening allure of Russian Roulette (one revolver, six chambers, one bullet...) is the sheer random danger, the fine line between life and death that's walked whenever the trigger is pulled.

Beer Roulette attempts to offer a similar thrill, but without the guns and the bullets. In short, one person takes an ordinary six-pack of beer/lager out of the room and shakes one of the cans. Not just a little shake. But a big, vigorous, very violent shake. Then the can is mixed up with the five unshaken cans and returned to the room, where all six are placed in a bag. One by one, the budding Beer Roulette players pick cans out of the bag and open them right under their noses. If yours is the beer that explodes, then you are considered 'dead', and must sit out the next round. The survivors then knock back their opened beers and the process begins anew. The last player 'alive' wins the game.

BOLLOXED FACTOR...

 Hints and Tips

It helps to make sure that the cans aren't very cold either. Take them out of the fridge **15 minutes** before needed.

Bottle Tops

058 More indiscriminate flicking. But this time, it's bottle tops.

ESSENTIAL SUPPLIES

BOTTLED BEER. SOME EXTRA BOTTLE TOPS.

You know the drill by now... gather a group of friends and sit everybody down in a big circle. Each player puts an open bottled beer in front of them, with the bottle top balanced neatly (upside down) on the top of the neck. Taking it in turns, the players then use extra bottle tops to try and knock the tops off of the bottles. Throw them, spin them, flick them... whatever way you launch the tops, if you knock the top off another player's beer, they must take a drink from it. Knock it off twice and not only does the player have to drink again, but you can make up a rule and a booze-tinted consequence if the rule is broken. Knock a player's bottle top off three times and the targeted player must finish his bottle in one go.

You can keep firing bottle tops at people's beer until you miss, whereupon your turn ends and the player to your left gets a go. At no time during the game can you adjust your bottle top if it is starting to slip. Illegal bottle-top intervention is punishable by a five-sip fine.

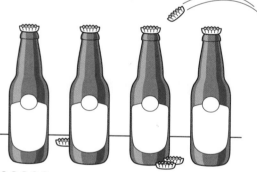

BOLLOXED FACTOR...

Hints and Tips

It can be a good idea to use more than just one bottle of beer each, particularly later on, when no one can aim straight.

Jugs

059 Sorry, lads. This game has absolutely nothing to do with breasts.

ESSENTIAL SUPPLIES

A LARGE JUG OR BOWL. A SMALL GLASS (A HALF-PINT ONE WILL DO). BEER.

This game, say its fans, is 'reminiscent of the game Spill the Beans but with an alcoholic twist'. Fill the large jug or bowl about three-quarters full of beer and then place the glass, also three-quarters full of beer, inside the jug. With any luck, the glass should now be floating inside the jug – if it sinks, it's too full, if it capsizes there's not enough beer to weight it down sufficiently.

The aim of the game is simply this: each player in turn tries to add some beer to the floating glass without sinking it. The unfortunate player who finally makes the glass sink must scoop out the glass, fill it with beer and drink the contents. Similarly, anybody jogging, nudging or bumping the table, which causes the glass to sink, gets penalised with a pint-of-beer fine.

Don't mention the war... but this game is also known as Sink the Bismarck in certain circles.

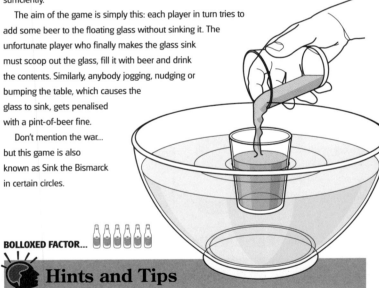

BOLLOXED FACTOR...

Hints and Tips

You're going to need quite a lot of beer to play this, so make sure you're well stocked up before the game starts.

Blind Ignorance

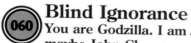

060 You are Godzilla. I am Japan. Or Bonaparte. Or maybe John Cleese...

ESSENTIAL SUPPLIES

CIGARETTE ROLLING PAPERS OR POST-IT NOTES. BEER.

A guessing game with a suitably adult twist, Blind Ignorance is great for all social occasions. Using Rizla papers or Post-It notes, each player writes down the name of a person (real or fictional). Then, turning to the person on their right, and WITHOUT showing that person the name of the person, stick the bit of paper on to their forehead.

The identity of everyone in the group is now plainly obvious, apart that is from your own as you can't see what has been written down and slapped on to your skull. Players have to take it in turns to ask key questions about the person that they are supposed to be, to which the other players can only answer 'yes' or 'no'. Guessing players can continue to ask questions e.g. 'Am I a man?' 'Am I a famous actor?' etc.) until they receive 'no' as an answer.

When this happens, their go then ends, and play passes to the next player, who attempts to guess his/her secret identity. Players who have successfully deciphered the clues and discovered the name of the personage scribbled on their forehead, can remove the name-revealing sticker from their heads. And the last person to work it out...? Rearrange 'finger', 'fine' and 'five' into a sentence to get your answer. If you want to make the game a little more 'exciting', you can make each player suffer a suitable penalty each time they ask a question and get 'no' as a reply. A couple of sips should be about right.

BOLLOXED FACTOR...

 Hints and Tips

Try and be imaginative when choosing a character. A good, sneaky one is to choose the person themselves. That's always hard to guess.

Dangerous Darts
The classic pub game, but without the serious intent.

ESSENTIAL SUPPLIES

A PUB DARTBOARD. DARTS. BEER.

Dangerous Darts, or Beer Darts, is a quick-and-easy game that favours both those with skill and dexterity, and those who just hurl the darts at the board hoping for the best.

Play evolves as follows: each player steps up to throw his/her three 'arrows' at the board. Scoring can continue as usual (or you can just forget all about it, the choice is yours), because it's not how much you score with your darts, it's where the darts land on the board that determines the penalties that the players incur. For example:

(1) If your dart lands in a black area, drink two-fingers/sips of beer.

(2) If your dart lands in a white area, breathe a sigh of relief and do nothing.

(3) If your dart misses the board completely and thwunks loudly into the wall, drink four fingers/sips — add an extra one if the dart falls to the floor and sticks in it.

(4) If your dart lands in the number 13, drink five fingers/sips.

(5) If your dart hits a 'double', your opponent must drink three fingers/sips from their pint.

(6) If your dart hits a 'triple', your opponent must drink four fingers/sips from their pint.

(7) If your dart hits the 'Bullseye', your opponent must drink four fingers/sips from their pint.

(8) If your dart lands in number 7, your opponent must drink seven fingers/sips from their pint.

BOLLOXED FACTOR...

Hints and Tips

You'll probably be tempted to aim for a lot of 7s, but make sure you look out for that dastardly 13 – it's not very far away.

Ice-Cube Raft Race

062 Just like the legendary pub relay, Boat Race, but on a much smaller scale.

ESSENTIAL SUPPLIES

AN ICE-CUBE TRAY. SHOTS OF YOUR FAVOURITE SPIRIT. SOME STRAWS.

Borrow an ice-cube tray from the bar/your kitchen, and fill the compartments with a spirit or strong beer. If it's a tray with two rows of sections, all the better as one player can take the left side, racing another player who takes the right.

The idea is to drink each compartment dry through a straw, before moving on to the next one, and then the next, until all of the compartments have been emptied. Whoever finishes first wins and condemns the loser to a forfeit of their choice.

Variant: Ice-Cube Relay Race. Try using two or three trays and two teams of players. Put the trays on different tables and make competing players run to the next table after they have drained the liquids out of their own tray. They then pass the straw on to the next player, who drinks each compartment in his/her own tray. Adding a line of peanuts that can only be eaten one-by-one with the player only allowed to use his/her mouth can be used to break things up.

BOLLOXED FACTOR...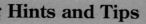

 Hints and Tips

Putting a different spirit in every cube can add a certain frisson to this already fairly lethal game – just work along the bar's optics.

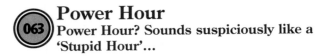

Power Hour
Power Hour? Sounds suspiciously like a 'Stupid Hour'...

ESSENTIAL SUPPLIES

LOTS OF BEER. TREMENDOUS STAMINA AND BLADDER CONTROL.

Although it's not really a game, the Power Hour is an endurance challenge, a game with no penalties, shouting, gesture-making, coin-spinning, card-holding or die-flipping. It's a test of a beer-drinker's manhood, an event, like a full Marathon, which should only be attempted once, just so you can say that you've done it. Here's how it works: quite simply, the Power Hour challenges you to swig a gulp of beer, every minute, for an entire hour. That's it. Sound easy? Can you make it through the time-limit without missing a gulp or going to the bathroom? Any break with the single Power Hour rule, and players will be penalised a whole pint of beer, which must be consumed within 30 seconds, so as not to further disrupt the vital gulp-per-minute schedule.

Variant: The Hundred Club: Uses the same basic idea as the Power Hour, but wannabe Hundred Club members swig a gulp of beer every minute for 100 minutes. Bloody fools.

BOLLOXED FACTOR...

Hints and Tips

Make sure you've got plenty of beer lined up. You don't want to waste time by having to go to the bar, do you?

Beer Square
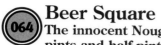

064 The innocent Noughts & Crosses becomes full pints and half-pints.

ESSENTIAL SUPPLIES

NINE BEER MATS. NINE PINTS OF BEER. TWO PLAYERS..

A beer-tinged version of the old Tic-Tac-Toe (Noughts & Crosses) game, the rules for Beer Square are concise and simple. Arrange your nine beer mats in a 3 x 3 square and decide which two players will go first. After this, each player takes it in turn to either put a pint of beer on the table or to drink from a pint of beer that's already on the table. The aim is to get three of a kind in a horizontal, vertical or diagonal row – i.e. three full pints, three half-full pints, or three empty glasses. Each turn, players can (a) drink half of a full pint, leaving a half-full glass on the table; (b) drink from a half-full pint, leaving an empty glass on the table; (c) add a pint glass to the 3 x 3 square, either leaving it full or drinking from it to create a half-full glass or an empty glass. Glasses must be replaced on the mat they were removed from. The winner is the person who organises the board so that there are three glasses of the same type in a row. The loser doesn't pay a drinking forfeit. But he/she does have to stump up for the next round. Nine beers please barman... ouch.

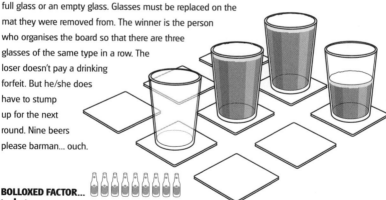

BOLLOXED FACTOR...

Hints and Tips

The player who forms a line of full pint glasses is the one who gets least drunk, and thus has the best chance to win.

Thumper

About as far away from Bambi's lovable bunny pal as you're likely to get.

ESSENTIAL SUPPLIES

LOTS OF BEER. A TABLE. A GOOD SENSE OF RHYTHM.

Although there is some wordplay in Thumper, the bulk of this fast-paced drinking game revolves around making silly gestures with hands, feet, torso – if you can move it, use it... To play, gather a group of open-minded people around a table.

To distinguish themselves from one another, each person must invent a gesture to represent him/her. When the gestures have been revealed (players should do this twice in an attempt to imprint the strange movements on the brains of the other players), everybody at the table should then start drumming on the surface with their fingers.

One player says: 'What is the name of the game?' To which everyone should reply in unison: 'Thumper!' The first player now says: 'Why do we play it?' To which everyone should gleefully yell: 'To get pissed'.

Now comes the tricky part... the first player then makes his gesture, followed by the gesture of one of the other players. The player to whom the second gesture belongs must quickly respond to this by flourishing their gesture, followed by another player's.

All the while everybody is drumming... Anybody who stops drumming must drink a suitable fine. Anybody who performs the wrong gesture, or gestures out of turn is also penalised. Players cannot make the gesture of the player immediately previous to their go. If they do, they face a double fine.

BOLLOXED FACTOR...

 ## Hints and Tips

Try and make your gesture fairly complicated. That way it won't be remembered so often – unless you like having to drink a lot.

Turbo Cups
066 Pass the plastic cup of beer in this pub-friendly relay race.

ESSENTIAL SUPPLIES: ONE CUP PER PLAYER. A TABLE. BEER.

A twisted relay race with beer, Turbo Cups requires two teams, each with three or four players.

Line up the teams on opposite sides of a handily placed table. Fill one cup per person with beer and arrange them in a neat row. The first member of each team must then approach the table. After somebody shouts 'Go!', these two players must drink their cup of beer as quickly as they can. Once finished, they must place the empty cup on the lip of the table, so that one half of the cup's base overhangs the edge. They must then, using their forefinger, flip the cup up on to the table, trying to make it land upside down. If the player succeeds, their go is over and the second player in the team can approach the table, drink his/her beer and attempt to flip over the next cup. Players must stay at the table, continually flipping the cup, for as long as it takes for it to land upside down. The first team to (a) drink all their beer and (b) to flip all their cups correctly wins the race.

Variant: Introduce a second round with three cups of beer per person. The first round takes place as normal, while the second requires players to drink and flip two cups.

BOLLOXED FACTOR...

Beat The Barman

067 An outrageous game that we suspect very few of you will actually play.

ESSENTIAL SUPPLIES

A FRIENDLY BARMAN. ARROGANCE. NO FEAR. MONEY.

A silly game, best played at the end of the night (when you should be high on Dutch Courage and therefore have the balls of an elephant), and in a pub where you and the barstaff are extremely good friends. If you don't, you face getting shouted at, beaten up, thrown out, arrested and, worst of all, barred. Because as far as the urban myth is concerned, nobody wins a game of Beat The Barman. Then again, nobody really loses or draws either. So, for all you buzz-craving, insane drinkers, here's how the game works:

(1) The player walks up to the bar and orders a short with no ice or lemon slices. (2) The crafty player then pays for said short with far too much money (3) While the barman nips back to the cash register to get the change, the player quickly downs the short, hides the glass and puts on a confused, yet innocent, smile. (4) When the barman returns with the change, go back to step (1).

Short on luck and skill, but big on confrontation, a game of Beat The Barman can end in several ways. Firstly, if the player falls over in a sorry, drunken heap, then the pub wins. If the barman visits any violence upon the player's person as a result of his/her cheekiness, then the game is considered drawn. Similarly, the game is also deemed drawn if the management eject the arrogant player from the pub and bar him for life. Finally, if the pub is closed as a result of the player's actions (not if last orders have been shouted and it's the accepted chucking-out time), then the drinker wins the day.

BOLLOXED FACTOR...

Hints and Tips

You should only contemplate getting involved in this game if you're astride a jet-powered motorbike on a highway to oblivion. Clearly.

Beer Bungee

068 Dangerous sports meets alcohol in the safest environment available – the beer garden.

ESSENTIAL SUPPLIES

A BUNGEE CORD. BEER.

Opportunities to play Beer Bungee don't pop up very often down your local. A 20ft bungee cord isn't exactly something that most barmen keep behind the crisps. That said, in most pubs, you'd be hard-pressed to find a clear 20ft to play the game in. In ideal circumstances, you should attach one end of the bungee to a pub door or wall, making sure there's a gap of about 30ft between the wall/door and the bar. But as this isn't always possible, Beer Bungee is best played in a garden. Tie the end of the bungee to a solid, heavy object (a tree, a truck, etc.) and place the glasses of beer on a table about 30ft away. Attach a player to the other end of the bungee and watch as they try to reach the beer on the table. Players should just about be able to reach it. But it's almost impossible to get it back without spilling it. Silly to play, but fun to watch.

BOLLOXED FACTOR...

Hints and Tips

The truly devious will place each drink slightly further away than the preceding one, with hilarious consequences.

Sixty Seconds

When clock-watching CAN be fun. Next time: we link drinking and watching paint dry...

ESSENTIAL SUPPLIES

A WATCH OR CLOCK WITH A SECOND HAND/DIGITAL DISPLAY. BEER.

Quick and easy – this is almost a fast-track to alcoholic oblivion. Sixty Seconds is another game that bases its drinking around random numbers. In this case, instead of cards, dice, money or characters in movies, all you need to play is an analogue clock (one with a second hand) or a good digital timepiece with a second-by-second count. To play, each player picks a selection of ten numbers between 1 and 60 (i.e. 1–10, 11–20, 31–40, and so on) and whenever the second hand/digital count reaches a player's set of numbers, that player has to keep drinking until the count passes by the last number in their sequence. And that's it. A good game if you're stuck in the middle of a watch factory, with no cards, dice, money or TV and have a large supply of beer to get through.

BOLLOXED FACTOR...

 Hints and Tips

It's probably best to hang the watch up somewhere so that there's no chance of it becoming beer-sodden and stopping.

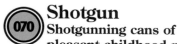

Shotgun

070 Shotgunning cans of beer. It's one of those pleasant childhood memories...

ESSENTIAL SUPPLIES

CANS OF BEER. A POINTY IMPLEMENT (A COMPASS POINT, SHARP KNIFE).

Another traditional party pastime, Shotgunning isn't really a drinking game in itself, but it can be adapted to fit in with many of the games in this book. Especially if used as a drinking penalty. For those of you who aren't familiar with the concept of shotgunning, here's a recap.

Grab a can of beer. But before you open it, carefully puncture a small hole near the bottom of the can with a knife, a fork prong or something suitable pointy and sharp. Then simply place your mouth over the hole (watch out for any sharp edges when you do this), raise your head up so the can is being held vertically and then open the can.

The pressurised beer will then be forced through the new hole at a tremendous rate, and the drinker must attempt to swallow it quickly without spilling any over their clothes, presuming they want to stay dry. The faster you drink, the more drunk you'll become (we find this is a rule that holds true for almost any kind of drinking endeavour). So surely this must be perfect as a fine for persistently bad games-players.

Variant: Shotgun Boat Race: Organise two teams into traditional Boat Race set ups (e.g. a line of four players, beer... you should remember the score from Turbo Cups on page 89). But instead of drinking pints one at a time and putting the empty glasses on your head, each player must shotgun a can, then crush it on the tabletop before the next player can start drinking... Funnily enough, the crushing bit tends to get easier as the evening wears on, but be careful not to damage any priceless antique furniture.

BOLLOXED FACTOR...

 Hints and Tips

You probably shouldn't try this with any of those extra-large party cans that some offies sell, but if you do – we salute you!

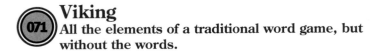

Viking

071 All the elements of a traditional word game, but without the words.

ESSENTIAL SUPPLIES

BEER. A KNOWLEDGE OF ANCIENT NORDIC HEADGEAR.

Another simple game quite similar in style to the way that wordgames function, with the obvious difference that nobody in a game of Viking is allowed to speak.

Here's how it works: The players (up to ten) sit in a circle and one person is chosen to start the game. This player quickly makes "Viking horns," created by sticking their thumbs in their ears and wiggling the remaining fingers. Then the player stops, claps his hands together once, and points at another person in the circle. This next player is also required to make the embarrassing sign of the Viking; the difference this time, however, is that the players either side of the new Viking also come into play and must 'steer the boat'. What this means is that the two flanking players must make a rowing action – the person on the left of the Viking rows to the left, the person on the right rows to the right. If all this happens quickly and correctly, the Viking can then stop wiggling his hands in his/her ears, clap hands and pass the Viking buck to another player.

Play repeats until either a Viking misses their cue, or one of the flanking rowers forgets to make the appropriate oaring action. Whoever misses their action must drink a penalty.

Variant: Bunnies: Instead of Viking horns, try floppy bunny ears with players putting two hands to their head and wiggling them like rabbit ears. When this happens, the player on the left must raise and waggle their right hand only, while the person on the right must waggle the left hand as an ear.

BOLLOXED FACTOR...

Hints and Tips

It's sensible to play this in a pub where you're well known. Your reputation will be amusingly enhanced for months afterwards.

Master of the Thumb

072 A diverting sub-game to liven up a hard night's drinking.

ESSENTIAL SUPPLIES

BEER.

This game can be played in conjunction with any other game featured in this book or as an extra rule during the course of an evening's gaming. The game starts by nominating a player to be the eponymous Master of the Thumb.

While it offers no advantages in the game that it's added to, the designated Master of the Thumb can certainly spice the night up by using the one special power that he/she possesses. In short, the digit-king can, at any time, place his/her thumb down on the edge of the table. If it is left there, anybody who notices that the thumb-master has placed a strategic thumb down, can emulate the move by placing their own thumb on the table.

The last person to notice the thumb movement loses this Master of the Thumb sub-game and is forced to drink a suitable penalty. The loser then becomes the new Master Of The Thumb and whatever game the group was originally playing, continues.

Variants: Master of the Nose: (the nasal chief can kick the process off by placing their forefinger on the end of their nose); **Arms Crossed** (the designated arm-crosser keeps their arms, er, crossed. The last one to notice and emulate, drinks); **Hands-On-Head** (fairly obvious, don't you think); and so on.

BOLLOXED FACTOR...

 Hints and Tips

When you're the master, try and use some other action to disguise what you're doing. Like standing up, raising yourself by the thumbs...

5 TONGUE TWISTERS AND WORD GAMES

Highly portable (all you need is your mouth, your brain and a couple of useful limbs), drinking games based on word association, spelling and name-calling are among the most popular boozy entertainment you can find. They can be played anywhere too because most of them don't require any props. So pick a game and try your luck. See how long it takes for your mouth to stop working and your hands to refuse to communicate with your head...

073 # I Never Did
A game that requires a keen mind and a low embarrassment threshold.

ESSENTIAL SUPPLIES

BEER. SPIRITS.

A simple, alcoholic version of the party favourite Truth or Dare – a game that will undoubtedly start off slow and cautious, but that just as inevitably gets better the longer you play and the more you drink...

Gather a group of friends around a table, or in a circle on the floor. Select one player to begin. This player kicks off the game by saying, 'I never did...' followed by something that the player actually has done. Everybody around the table who also has done the exploit mentioned by the speaking player then drinks an appropriate drinking fine. Then the next player announces that he/she 'never did' something and play continues around the circle. As the inhibitions start to crumble due to excessive alcohol consumption later in the game, the deeds mentioned will alter from the largely innocent ('I never did go to the supermarket'), to the risky ('I never did lie and say I was busy') to the downright confrontational, ('I never did sleep with Dave's wife').

BOLLOXED FACTOR...

 ## Hints and Tips

Don't ever play this game with anyone you've really done something terrible – and secret – to. It'll come out...

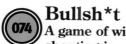

Bullsh*t

A game of wits, finesse and loud, uncouth shouting in public places.

ESSENTIAL SUPPLIES

BEER. SPIRITS.

As usual, for this fast-paced, slightly bawdy word game, gather a group of friends together in a circle or around a table, and select one of the players to go first. This player kicks off the game by announcing: 'One day I was walking down the street when I saw [name of player two] taking a shit!' Player two then counters loudly with: 'Bullshit!' Quickly player one chips in with: 'Who shit?' to which player two adds "[name of player three] shit". Now it's player three's turn to say 'Bullshit!' Player two then says 'Who shit?' to which player three can then say '[name of player four] shit'. Once the game has completed a circle of the players involved, the players can nominate any player in the circle in any order. Penalties are awarded for hesitation, for speaking out of turn or for slurring your words. To make things more difficult, try the game by assigning different names to the players, i.e. player one, player two, etc; or celebrity names, animal names, and so on. The only other rules are that if two people duel verbally with each other for more than three times then they both have to drink. And if a player mucks up his/her go more than three times, they are condemned to finish the rest of their beer/short.

BOLLOXED FACTOR...

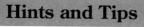

Hints and Tips

> This is another game where you need to be careful about who's overhearing you. Potential girlfriends are not going to be impressed.

Actor & Movie

075 A simple game of movie knowledge enlivened by a smattering of lovely booze.

ESSENTIAL SUPPLIES

BEER. SPIRITS. A LOOSE TONGUE.

Another simple knowledge game, where 'you either know it or you don't' and if 'you don't' you'll get into alcoholic trouble quicker than everybody else. This game's theme is the movies and although the rules of play are simple, an extensive knowledge of films, actors and actresses is a distinct advantage.

Here's how it works: gather a group of players and select somebody to go first. This player then names an actor or an actress and the rest of the players, in turn, attempt to name a film that the named actor/actress has been in (30 seconds are allowed for deep thought). So, if player one says 'Bill Pullman', player two could mention '*Independence Day*', player three might say '*Lost Highway*' and so on. The first person who can't guess a movie that the relevant star has appeared in, or says a movie that the star did NOT appear in, has to drink a penalty.

And there's a neat twist – when somebody can't think of a movie the actor/actress has appeared in, the other players get 60 seconds to try and think of some extra ones. The total of these films is counted up after the minute has passed and the player paying the penalty must then drink for X seconds (where X is the number of films that the other players managed to think of).

Unsurprisingly, a keen knowledge of little-known Euro-actors and arthouse is a distinct advantage. Everybody can name some movies that Bruce Willis has been in. But how many people will be able to list the filmography of Kôji Yakusho?

BOLLOXED FACTOR...

 Hints and Tips

Watch lots of Wim Wenders films and buy a huge movie guide if you want to be any good at this diabolically difficult game.

Categories

076 Think, drink. Think, drink. Repeat until 'sober' sounds like 'sofa'.

ESSENTIAL SUPPLIES

BEER. SPIRITS.

Another relatively simple game, worth learning because it can be used as part of the Multi card-based drinking game. Gather people together in a rough circle and select an eager player to go first. He/she must think of an appropriate category, e.g. British football teams, and then each subsequent player must name an item/thing that fits into the category – so player two could say 'Manchester United', player three might mumble 'Liverpool' and so on. Hesitation is punishable with a drinking penalty, as is the player who can't think of a new item/thing to add to the category. This player then drinks the penalty and chooses a new category. Then the game begins anew. Told you it was simple.

Variants: A Ship Came Into the Harbour: The same game, but with a salty, nautical spin. The first player announces that: 'a ship came into the harbour carrying... a cargo of beer', then the players around the table must name different brands of beer or lager (Heineken, Kronenbourg, Carlsberg, etc.) Whoever can't think of a new kind of beer, then pays the penalty and picks a new category, e.g. 'A ship came into the harbour carrying... a cargo of cigarettes.'

BOLLOXED FACTOR...

 Hints and Tips

Try and choose relatively easy categories, because the game is more fun played like that. 'Mongolian Cheeses' is not clever.

Buzz

077 A fun and simple drinking game that tests those long-forgotten maths skills.

ESSENTIAL SUPPLIES

BEER. SPIRITS.

This well-known game may sound easy to play, but its simplicity is merely a smokescreen for a devilish word game that's actually much trickier than it first appears. Start the game by sitting everyone down in a circle and by picking one player to start. This player then begins to count, saying the number 'One'. The person to their immediate left then says 'Two', the next player says 'Three', and so on around the group.

Things start to get interesting, however, when the count gets to either 7, 11, a multiple of 7 or 11, or a number that features 7 in its digits. As soon as this happens, the player must say 'Buzz' instead of the number, e.g. 1, 2, 3, 4, 5, 6, Buzz, 8, 9, 10, Buzz, 12, 13, Buzz, 15, etc.)

Also, as soon as someone says 'Buzz', you switch directions – so if the game was rolling to the left, it now stops, reverses and moves around to the right. Again, if anybody hesitates, says a 7, 11, multiple of 7 or 11, or a number with 7 in it, or says 'Buzz' when they don't have to, the usual drinking penalty (for example, two fingers/sips per mistake) applies. Easy to learn, difficult to master, repeat the game, getting faster and faster, until the participants can no longer stand, let alone count from 1–10.

Variants: Fizz Buzz: This version plays in the same way as Buzz above, only that instead of numbers containing or divisible by 7 and 11, the game challenges players by changing the magic number to 3. That means that no number that's a multiple of 3 or features a 3 can be said. Instead the player must substitute the numeral with either 'Buzz' or 'Fizz' – e.g. 1, 2, Fizz, 4, 5, Buzz, 7, 8, Buzz, etc. Simply put, if a player says 'Buzz' the direction of play reverses, but if the player says 'Fizz' the play continues in the same direction. Any mistake is penalised by a drink. Believe it, this can get incredibly confusing.

Bizz Buzz Bang: Now it gets really tricky. Bizz Buzz Bang takes the obvious step and introduces different words for different numbers and their multiples. In this case, Bizz equals 3, Buzz represents 5 and Bang takes the place of 7. So whenever a 3 or a multiple of 3 comes up during the count, you say 'Bizz' (3, 6, 9, 12, 13, 15, etc.); whenever a 5 or multiple of 5 comes up, you say 'Buzz' (5, 10, 15, 20, etc.); and when a 7 or multiple of 7 comes up, you say 'Bang' (7, 14, 17, 21, 27, 28 etc.)

Finally, if you have a number that has more than two properties, you say both words – e.g. 15 is divisible by 3 and 5 so you would say 'Bizz-Buzz'; 35 contains a 3, and is divisible by 5 and 7, so this warrants a 'Bizz-Buzz-Bang'. Thus, a game would unfold like this: 1, 2, Bizz, 4, Buzz, Bizz, Bang, 8, Bizz, Buzz, 11, Bizz, Bizz, Bang, Bizz-Buzz, 16, and so on. As usual, anybody who makes a mistake, drinks. If anyone can work out that they have.

BOLLOXED FACTOR...

Hints and Tips

We can't help you here. All we suggest is that you try and work a little bit ahead so that you have some idea what's coming. It won't last long.

Drink Don't Think
By far this author's favourite drinking game. Fun, demanding and deadly...

ESSENTIAL SUPPLIES

BEER. SPIRITS.

Typically simple yet addictively playable, Drink Don't Think is one of the easiest/trickiest drinking games ever devised. And that's just the start of the seriously twisted thinking that this game is going to inspire in you.

Here's how it works: gather your group of friends and select a player to go first. This player then kicks off the game by saying the name of a famous person, either a celebrity (Johnny Depp, Bruce Willis) or a well-known cartoon character (Donald Duck, Mickey Mouse).

The next player to go can then say the name of another celebrity, a name that must begin with the first letter of the previous celeb's surname. For example, player one might start with Paris Hilton, so player two would have to say a name beginning with 'H', such as Hilary Clinton. Player three therefore has to think of a name that begins with a 'C', Charles Dance, and so on.

The extra rules are simple: while a player thinks of a name he/she has to continually sip from their drink; if a player says a name that has a surname and a forename that begin with the same letter, i.e. Charlie Chaplin, the direction of play is reversed. Names cannot be reused or repeated, if this happens the offending player must down the rest of their drink. Finally, players that cannot think of a name, must drink a two-finger/sip penalty. Continue forever.

BOLLOXED FACTOR...

Hints and Tips

Panic is the enemy in this game. Above all else just try and stay completely, utterly calm. Otherwise you're going to lose it big-time.

Fuzzy Duck

079 Fuzzy Duck? Reverse the D and the F and giggle at the rudeness of it all...

ESSENTIAL SUPPLIES

BEER. SPIRITS.

Herd your favoured friends into a circle and spin a coin to decide who goes first (preferably somebody who knows how to play the game). Player one starts the game by saying: 'Fuzzy Duck'. The person to the left, player two, follows this opening gambit by either announcing: 'Fuzzy Duck' or 'Does he?' If the player plumps for saying 'Fuzzy Duck', the game continues and moves on to player three, who also has the opportunity to say 'Fuzzy Duck' or 'Does he?' If, however, a player decides to say 'Does he?', play is reversed (moving anticlockwise) and instead of 'Fuzzy Duck', players have to say 'Ducky Fuzz'. If a player says 'Does he?' again, the direction changes back and 'Ducky Fuzz' returns to the original 'Fuzzy Duck'.

Players drink a penalty if they say 'Fuzzy Duck' when they should say 'Ducky Fuzz' (and vice versa) or if they speak out of turn. Or, indeed, if they accidentally say something rude.

BOLLOXED FACTOR...

Hints and Tips

Somebody may latch on to the idea that it's clever to say 'Does he?' a lot. Well, it's not if everyone else does.

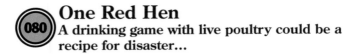

One Red Hen

080 A drinking game with live poultry could be a recipe for disaster...

ESSENTIAL SUPPLIES

BEER. SPIRITS.

Friends. Circle. You know the drill by now. Most importantly, however, players must nominate a 'leader', whose responsibility it is to memorise the sentences (in order) below.

> To the judge, King, and country!
> One red hen and a couple of ducks.
> Three brown bear.
> Four running hare.
> Five frolicking fillies.
> Six simple Simons.
> Seven salty seamen, sailing the seven seas.
> Eight elongated elephants elevating elegantly in an elevator.
> Nine nimble nymphomaniacs kneeling nicely in their nighties in a nunnery.
> Ten, I am not a fig plucker, nor a fig plucker's son. But, I'll pluck figs till the fig plucking's done.

Here's how it works: each of the lines must be repeated by the players after the leader has said them. Then they must take a drink. For example, the leader starts by saying tTo the judge, King, and country!' [takes a drink]. Everybody then takes it in turn to repeat this first sentence, taking a sip of drink afterwards. Then the leader says the second line. The other players must then repeat the whole passage thus far, i.e. 'To the judge, Queen, and country! One red hen, and a couple of ducks.' Then the leader says the third line on its own. Again, the other players must then repeat the whole passage with everybody taking a quick swig of drink after each one. Anyone who gets a sentence incorrect, or in the wrong order, must finish the rest of their drink (at least half-a-pint). The game continues until players have managed to say the full ten-line passage correctly.

BOLLOXED FACTOR...

Sentences

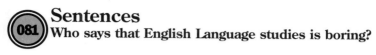

081 Who says that English Language studies is boring?

ESSENTIAL SUPPLIES

BEER. SPIRITS.

Circle of friends in place, leading player nominated, a game of Sentences (a tricky word game that's much more difficult than its simplistic rules suggest) can begin. Player one kicks things off by saying a random word. The next player must then say a word that helps form a sentence but doesn't finish it. The next player must do the same and so on around the group.

For example, in a four-player game: player one says 'Fish'; player two says 'love'; player three says 'swimming'; player four says 'in', player one says 'the'; player two says 'deep'; player three says 'blue'; player four says 'sea' and the game ends.

Play continues around the circle until somebody either: (a) says a word that doesn't make sense in the context of the sentence, (b) hesitates too long, (c) is the third person to add an adjective or (d) accidentally finishes the sentence. When this happens, the losing player drinks a suitable boozy forfeit. Play then begins with a new word.

BOLLOXED FACTOR...

Hints and Tips

'And' can become such a useful and eventually irritating word that you may want to ban it from the start.

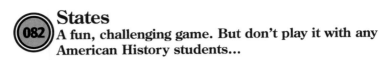

States
A fun, challenging game. But don't play it with any American History students...

ESSENTIAL SUPPLIES

BEER. SPIRITS.

There are two versions of this game and for the Brits, the simplest one (Guess The States) is probably the best. As usual, it involves a group of players and a nominated leader. The idea is simply to name each one of the 50 US states – easy for our American cousins, perhaps, but slightly tricky for the rest of us. Player one begins by mentioning a state, e.g. Texas, and play continues until a player either cannot think of a new state or says a state that has already been referenced. Naturally, the loser drinks an appropriate fine – a half-a-pint of beer or a shot.

Variants: Counties: The idea is to name England's counties. Play continues until a player either cannot think of a new county or repeats one. The usual fine applies to the loser.

Um, States: Like States before it, Um, States is a simple game that works best if played with people that don't know the following rule. It is this: play moves around the circle naming US states, but to get your guess right, you have to add an 'um' before you mention the name. If you don't, you are not aware of the pattern and must drink a forfeit. Players that know the pattern can repeat states as long as they use an 'um' or make up new states. Anything goes as long as there's an 'um'. Play ends when the players who didn't know the rules finally crack the pattern.

Scissors States: Like Um, States, but instead of adding the word 'um' in front of the name of the state, you say the name of the state (or a made-up area) with your arms casually crossed. Anybody who doesn't know the rules has to drink. Ha-ha.

BOLLOXED FACTOR...

 Hints and Tips

Swotty, boring types may want to gen up on the names of all the states. Let them do it, but don't let them ever play again...

083 Bouncing Ball

A game played with an invisible ball. Yet after 16 pints, you might be able to see it!

ESSENTIAL SUPPLIES

BEER. SPIRITS. AN IMAGINARY BALL.

A game that uses elements of Buzz and Fizz Buzz, Bouncing Ball is a fast-paced word game that's best played with a reasonably large group of players, e.g. six. As usual, get a load of friends together, some beer and sit everybody around a table or in a rough circle in a variety of comfy chairs.

The basic rule of the game is this: only three words can be spoken once the game begins – 'Whizz', 'Bounce', and 'Boing'. Next, pick somebody to start the game. This person holds the imaginary ball, which will move around the group depending on which of the three words the players say.

If a player says 'Whizz' the ball passes on to the next player.

If a player says 'Bounce', the ball skips the next player and bounces on to the following player.

Finally, if a player says 'Boing', the ball reverses direction.

So in a sample game, it would work like this. Play begins with player one who says 'Whizz'; player two gets the ball and says 'Boing' sending it back to player one; player one now gets the ball and says 'Boing' to send the ball back to player two; player two says 'Whizz' to give it to player three; player three says 'Bounce' to skip player four and move on to player one. And so on. Drinking penalties are incurred if any player hesitates, or says a word when he/she doesn't have the ball or passes the ball the wrong way.

BOLLOXED FACTOR...

 Hints and Tips

As with any of the word games in this chapter, the faster you play this game, the more fun you'll be certain to have.

Ibble-Dibble
084 A fine fast-paced drinking game with silly words and strange props.

ESSENTIAL SUPPLIES

BEER. SPIRITS. A CORK. A LIGHTER (OR BOX OF MATCHES).

Arrange a gang of players around a table and assign each one of these players a number. So, assuming there are four players, assign numbers 1–4 to the people around the table in a clockwise direction.

Make sure everybody has at least one large drink, then take the cork and blacken one end of it by burning it with the lighter or the matches. Now for the game... First of all, it's vital that you understand these two basic concepts – an 'Ibble-dibble' is a player who wants to get drunk; a 'dibble-ibble' is a black mark on a player's face made by the cork. Once you understand this, you can start to play the game.

Whoever has been assigned the number 1 kicks off the game and can pass the play on to anybody else in the circle by naming himself (i.e. 'number one ibble-dibble' – player one who wants to get drunk), identifying how many marks he has ('with no dibble-ibbles' – no cork marks), and then calling another player and identifying the number of marks they have ('calling number 3 ibble-dibble with 1 dibble-ibble' – player three who wants to get drunk and has one mark).

So, a sample game might go something like this: player one says: 'This is number one ibble-dibble with no dibble-ibbles calling number three ibble-dibble with no dibble-ibbles'; player three would then quickly respond with: 'This is number three ibble-dibble with no dibble-ibbles calling number four ibble-dibble with no dibble-ibbles'. If player three had

BOLLOXED FACTOR...

 Hints and Tips

Try not to have too far to travel home after you've been playing this. No cab is going to stop for someone covered in dibble-ibbles.

paused, he/she would have a sooty mark added to their face and has to drink a penalty. Then the player can continue; 'This is number three ibble-dibble with one dibble-ibble calling number two ibble-dibble with no dibble-ibbles'. And so on. Drinking penalties are incurred for hesitation, or for getting your number of marks (dibble-ibbles) wrong, or for getting your dibble-ibbles and your ibble-dibbles mixed up.

Sergeant Major General
A fast-paced, name-calling game with a macho military theme.

085

ESSENTIAL SUPPLIES

BEER. SPIRITS.

Another simple word game, which involves calling people names for amusement. Specifically, once you've gathered a sizable group of friends around (say about six), these players are given ranks. Nominate a starting player and, moving clockwise around the group, dub player one the 'General', player two the 'Major', player three the 'Sergeant', player four '1', player five '2', and player 6 the 'Dunce'. The game is kicked off by the General, who calls out his own rank, followed by the rank of another player, e.g. General One, or General Major. Quickly, the player referenced in the previous player's call must pass the play onwards by calling out their own rank followed by somebody else's number. For example:

The General: General One

Player One: One Major

The Major: Major Sergeant

And so on...

The only real rule is that the game cannot be passed on to a player who is (a) sat either side of the caller, or (b) to the player that just gave the game to you. Anybody who speaks at the wrong time, or hesitates when called, drinks an appropriate forfeit. This loser then becomes the Dunce, who must sit in the Dunce's seat, and the rest of the players swap seats and ranks accordingly.

BOLLOXED FACTOR...

Hints and Tips

Try and decide what you're going to say before your rank is called out. Boy scouts should find this game particularly easy.

Like Pissed

086 It doesn't get any simpler and wilder than this.

ESSENTIAL SUPPLIES

BEER. SPIRITS.

Like Pissed is a simple, one-off game of no real skill whatsoever. What it relies on is the players' knowledge of words that mean 'drunk'. Gather your favourite drinking partners together around a table and then, with drinks in hand, take it in turn to name a word or phrase that is a slang synonym for inebriation. We've listed some examples below:

Shedded, Slaughtered, Bladdered, Tanked, Rat-arsed, Under the Table, Shit-faced, Had one too Many, Merry, Tipsy, Intoxicated, Boozed-up, Seeing Double, Wasted, Slammed, Off Yer Trolley, Half-Cut, Squiffy, Plastered, Sozzled, Sloshed, Screwed, Oiled, Beered-up, Lagered-up, Blind Drunk, Three Sheets to the Wind, Drunk as a Lord, Ripped, Trashed, Hammered, Skunked, Gooned, Pissed Out of your Tree, Sauced, Loaded, Annihilated, Bolloxed... and so on.

Anybody who can't think of a word or phrase must drink the usual forfeit. If any player offers a word that the others challenge, the group can put it to a vote to decide its validity.

BOLLOXED FACTOR...

 Hints and Tips

This game won't last forever, so have another one ready and prepared for when it all starts to peter out...

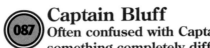

Captain Bluff

087 Often confused with Captain Snuff. But that's something completely different.

ESSENTIAL SUPPLIES

BEER. SPIRITS.

Again the ingredients are: a group of friends, beer and a table. Nominate a player to be the first Captain Bluff. This player then starts the game by saying: 'Captain Bluff takes his first drink.' After this the player picks up his beer with one finger and thumb, takes one sip, places the beer back on the table, tapping it once, winks once, pinches his left ear with his left hand once, his right ear with his right hand once, stands up and turns around once, before sitting down again. The other players must repeat this procedure exactly.

    If everyone succeeds, Captain Bluff then announces: 'Captain Bluff takes his second drink', following this with another suitably strange collection of gestures, which the players must then repeat. Anybody who fails gets a drinking penalty and must try to emulate Captain Bluff's movements again.

BOLLOXED FACTOR...

Hints and Tips

If Captain Bluff loses track of what he's done, it's time for a new Captain. 'Mutiny, Mr Christian?' Too right.

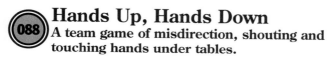

Hands Up, Hands Down

088 A team game of misdirection, shouting and touching hands under tables.

ESSENTIAL SUPPLIES

BEER. SPIRITS. A COIN.

This game requires two teams of at least three players, facing across from each other with a table between them. One team holds their hands face up in the air, about chest level with one member holding a coin that's visible to both teams.

When a player on the opposing team (the announcer) yells 'Hands down!', the team with the coin thrust their hands under the table, where they can secretly pass it between each other, hoping to fool the other team.

After a time, the announcer yells, 'Hands up!' and the coin-holding team, clench their fists (one holding the coin) and return them to the chest-height position. The announcer on the opposite team yells, 'Hands down!' and, in unison and while shouting 'Haa!' (to mask the sound of the coin), the coin-holders slam their hands down on the table, concealing the coin. Starting from the right, the opposite team attempts to guess which hand the coin is in by touching one of the opposing team's hands. The person touched must open his hand. If the coin is found, the coin-holding team takes a drink. If not, the guessing team drinks.

BOLLOXED FACTOR...

Animal

089 Enlightening gaming. For example, how exactly do you act 'like a bat'?

ESSENTIAL SUPPLIES

BEER. SPIRITS.

With a group of friends sat around a table, encourage each potential player to think of an animal, plus a noise and an action that will define that animal to the other players – e.g. a snake might be a hiss and a stuck-out tongue; a monkey might be a screech, illustrated by a player banging their fists on his/her chest.

To play the game, make sure that all of the players know what animals the others have chosen and pick a player to start. This player then makes his/her distinctive animal action and the accompanying noise, then the action and noise of another player's animal. This next player then performs his/her animal action and noise, plus that of another player in the circle. This continues around the circle. Drinking penalties are incurred if a player hesitates or if players get another player's animal action or noise incorrect.

BOLLOXED FACTOR...

  Hints and Tips

Once again, the faster you play this game, the better. Expect other people in the pub to be highly amused, as well.

6 TV, MOVIE AND SPORT-BASED GAMES

Like their card-, dice- and coin-based cousins, drinking games based on TV shows, movies or sports rely on the random element to dish out the beer-related penalties. Simply check the essential supplies to see exactly what you'll need, pick a character (if told to do so) and drink when an action or a quote appears from the lists here. That's all there is to it. Adding a drinking element to some of your favourite shows gives the night a refreshing, woozy twist.

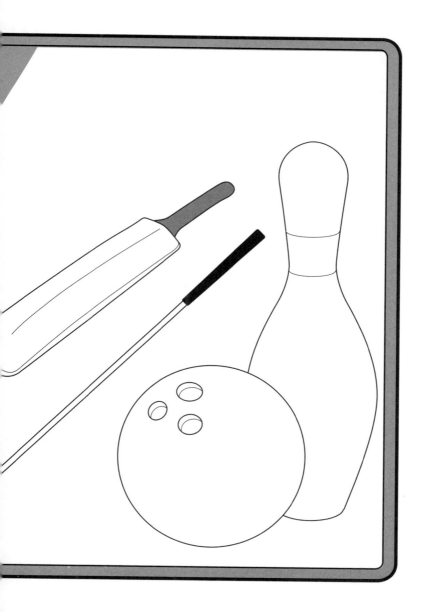

 The Star Wars Trilogy Drinking Game.

Rumour has it that Obi-Wan Kenobi could drink ten pints of Tattooine ale a night...

ESSENTIAL SUPPLIES

STAR WARS, THE EMPIRE STRIKES BACK, RETURN OF THE JEDI. BEER. LOTS OF FREE TIME.

Watch *Star Wars, The Empire Strikes Back* or *Return of the Jedi* and take a good old swig from your beer when any of the following happens on the screen.

·Someone has a bad feeling about this.

·It's their only hope.

·An entire planet is described as having one climate.

·Somebody gets choked.

·A woman other than Leia is on screen.

·An old Jedi starts to ramble about the Force.

·Somebody's hand/arm gets cut off.

·There is a tremor in the Force.

·It's not someone's fault.

·One or more heroes are almost eaten by a large alien 'thing'.

·Someone exclaims, 'No!'

·Someone wears the same outfit in all three movies.

·Someone is mind-controlled using the Force.

·A good guy wears white/a bad guy wears black.

·An alien character has lines in its original language (with or without subtitles).

·A spacecraft crashes into something after being hit by laser fire.

·A light sabre is used.

·An Ewok dies, and the camera lingers on it for dramatic effect.

·Luke whines.

·Luke fights monsters or savages.

BOLLOXED FACTOR...

·Luke performs an impossible acrobatic tumble/flip.

·Luke is upside down.

·Luke and Lando are onscreen at the same time.

·Luke refuses to take someone's advice.

·Leia insults somebody.

·Leia wears an outfit that covers everything except her face and hands.

·A see-through Obi-Wan Kenobi appears to offer advice.

·Han boasts about the capabilities of the Millennium Falcon.

·Somebody insults the capabilities of the Millennium Falcon.

·Despite its capabilities, something doesn't work on the Millennium Falcon.

·C3-PO loses a body part.

·C3-PO brags how many forms of communication he's familiar with.

·A Rebel Pilot says, 'Nice Shot...'

·A Rebel Pilot says, 'I've been hit...'

·Any Imperial Ship is destroyed.

·A Rebel ship is destroyed.

·Grand Moff Tarkin boasts about the awesome capabilities of the Death Star.

·The Emperor cackles evilly.

·The Emperor has foreseen something.

·The Emperor fires lightning bolts from his hands (keep drinking while the lightning continues).

·Boba Fett speaks.

·A Stormtrooper, despite the fact that he's wearing body armour, gets hit once by a laser blast and dies. Drink twice if he falls from a high place.

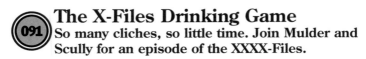

The X-Files Drinking Game

091 So many cliches, so little time. Join Mulder and Scully for an episode of the XXXX-Files.

ESSENTIAL SUPPLIES

AS MANY EPISODES OF THE SPOOKY TV SERIES YOU CAN FIND. BEER.

Pop an episode into the video (the ones that feature the alien subplot are particularly effective) and take a drink every time one of the following events occurs.

Take one swig from your drink when:

·Scully is called to do a post-mortem or examines a corpse.

·Mulder or Scully gets a call on their mobile phones from their partner.

·A powerful torch is waved in a very dark, slightly dusty room.

·Mulder mentions that something could be alien/paranormal/mystical etc. and another character thinks he's joking.

·Mulder mentions that something could be alien/paranormal/mystical etc. and Scully counters with a scientific explanation.

·Mulder mentions an old case with a similar theme that's almost directly related to the case that they're working on.

·Mulder and Scully split up to follow separate leads. Scully's lead proves to be a waste of time and she misses the alien/paranormal finale and doesn't believe Mulder when he tells her about it.

·A mysterious character shows up at the end of an episode to keep Mulder from learning the truth.

·A mysterious character shows up at the end of an episode to save Mulder's life.

Take two swigs from your drink when:

·Someone knows something about Mulder's sister. But they won't tell him about it.

·You spot the numbers 11/21, which correspond to the birthday of Chris Carter's wife...

·Mulder is called by his first name, Fox.

·Cancer Man lights a cigarette.

·Mulder mentions that his sister was abducted when he was very young.

BOLLOXED FACTOR...

·Someone calls Mulder 'Spooky Mulder'.

·Deep Throat or Mr X appears, complains that they should stop meeting like this, and tells Mulder absolutely nothing of importance.

·Mulder and Scully get into a fight.

Take three swigs from your drink when:

·A UFO appears or something paranormal happens in Scully's presence and she finds it difficult to explain.

·Scully ventures into dark place on her own.

·An alien appears (dead, frozen, running around, etc.)

·The shapeshifting aliens appear.

·Someone brandishes one of those retractable ice picks.

·A local sheriff helps the FBI in their investigation.

Then there's the much, much shorter X-Files Drinking Game. Which goes like so:

·Mulder or Scully uses a flashlight (one finger/sip).

·Mulder or Scully shows a badge and says "FBI" (one finger/sip).

·Mulder gets in a fist fight (one finger/sip).

·An alien appears (one finger/sip).

·Cancer Man appears (two fingers/sips).

·Mulder thinks about or makes reference to his sister (two fingers/sips).

·Someone says 'The Truth is Out There' (two fingers/sips).

·Scully is called away before the climax and therefore misses the overwhelming evidence that aliens/ghosts/large man worms/ witchcraft, etc. exists. (three fingers/sips).

The Roxanne Drinking Game

092 You wouldn't think that a three-minute song could get you plastered. But you'd be wrong...

ESSENTIAL SUPPLIES

A COPY OF THE POLICE'S FAMOUS SONG, 'ROXANNE'. BEER.

Oh-so-simple, yet oh-so-deadly. Dig up a copy of the Police tune 'Roxanne', bung it on the record player or in your CD system (or on the jukebox in your local) and drink every time you hear the band sing 'Roxanne'. Surprisingly, that's all there is to it. We guarantee you'll be amazed at how many times the word 'Roxanne' actually turns up. It's a hell of a lot.

BOLLOXED FACTOR...

 Hints and Tips

This admirable game can be easily converted to other songs. 'War', 'Delilah', 'Pump Up The Volume', etc., etc.

The James Bond Drinking Game
093 Another simple game – easy on the brain, heavy on the beer.

ESSENTIAL SUPPLIES

ANY OF THE JAMES BOND FILMS ON VIDEO. BEER.

You know the drill by now... Pop any one of the James Bond movies into your video and start watching. The rules, such as they are here, are ludicrously simple: every time that a character in the movie says 'James', drink twice from your beverage of choice; every time that a character in the movie says 'Bond', sip three times from your drink. Finally every time that someone says 'James Bond', drink half of your drink in one go and cheer happily. Like The Roxanne Drinking Game, the idea behind this alcoholic Bondage is fairly straightforward, but you'll be surprised how many times that 007's name will crop up. Watch out for the megalomaniac villains, who revel in saying 'Bond' more times than most, and the drop-their-dresses-on-the-floor girls who whisper 'Oh, James' before being relegated to a plot device. Try it for yourself and see how you go.

BOLLOXED FACTOR...

 Hints and Tips

You can always drink dry vodka martinis, prepared in that special way, if you want a little bit more authenticity.

094 The Simpsons Drinking Games 1 and 2

The world's most famous cartoon family gets given a hazy, booze-related twist.

ESSENTIAL SUPPLIES

A VAST HAUL OF SIMPSONS EPISODES. BEER.

There are two versions of The Simpsons Drinking Game. First up is The Simpsons Drinking Game 1 – pick a character and imbibe some alcohol if they get caught doing any following actions:

Homer Simpson

·Says 'Doh!' (drink twice if somebody else uses his famous catchphrase).

·Eats donuts, talks about donuts, sees donuts, dreams about donuts.

·Drools uncontrollably.

·Has a conversation with his own brain.

·Drinks some Duff beer.

Lisa Simpson

·Mentions humanity, the environment, truth, justice or the American way.

·Reads *Junior Sceptic* magazine.

·Plays the saxophone.

Bart Simpson

·Makes a crank phone call to Moe.

·Says 'Ay Carumba!'

·Wears something other than his usual top and shorts.

Marge Simpson

·Her towering blue hair casts a giant shadow.

BOLLOXED FACTOR...

·She says 'Homey'.

·She kisses Homer.

·She growls at Homer.

·She makes the family tea and defends her husband.

Maggie Simpson

·She falls down.

·She removes her dummy for a moment.

·Says a word (drink your whole pint if this happens, plus all of the beer you have in the house!)

Marge's sisters

·If they appear in a scene together (drink triple if one of them appears on their own).

·They smoke.

·They criticise Homer.

Ned Flanders:

·Mentions God, religion, the Church or says 'Okely-Dokely'.

For The Simpson's Drinking Game 2, just follow the list below:

·Pets make an appearance (one finger/sip)

·Barney Drinks (one finger/sip)

·Springfield Police corruption is revealed or the cops fail to catch a criminal (one finger/sip)

·Homer eats a donut (one finger/sip)

·Dr. Hibbert laughs (one finger/sip)

·Troy McLure says 'Hi, I'm Troy McLure' (one finger/sip)

·Bart rides his skateboard (one finger/sip)

·Flanders says 'Hidely-ho neighbor' (one finger/sip)

·Patty/Selma light a cigarette (one finger/sip)

·Nelson says 'Haah-haah' (one finger/sip)

·Evil nuclear power plant boss Mr. Burns says, 'excellent' (one finger/sip)

·Any Flanders member makes a reference to God (one finger/sip)

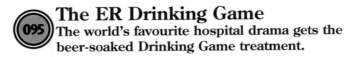

The ER Drinking Game

095 The world's favourite hospital drama gets the beer-soaked Drinking Game treatment.

ESSENTIAL SUPPLIES

LOTS OF ER EPISODES. BEER.

The ER Drinking Game operates on similar rules to other themed games – if any of the actions below occur onscreen, you must pay the drinking penalty specified. So, simply pick a character, settle down with a tape of the show, and prepare for action. Take a drink if any of your characters do any of the actions listed here:

If you picked Dr Greene, take a drink every time that:

·He cheats on wife (early episodes only).

·He goes out with someone from the ER.

·He doesn't wear his green ER scrubs.

·He tries to leave the ER at the end of the shift, but is held up by a new emergency that he just HAS to deal with.

·He manages to say, 'Goodnight' and leaves the ER.

·He encourages or gives some advice to a fellow worker.

·He forgets an important appointment because he is too busy saving lives in the ER.

·He goes against one of Dr Weaver's 'recommendations'.

If you picked Dr Carter, take a drink every time that:

·He acts like Dr Benton.

·He flirts with a female member of staff.

·We see Dr Carter's grandmother.

·He says something sarcastic about Benton.

·He learns a new procedure or technique.

·He saves a patient (drink triple if he loses a patient).

·He has an encounter with a medical student.

·He is the victim of a practical joke.

BOLLOXED FACTOR...

·He acts cooler than he actually is.

·He calls for a consult.

If you picked Dr Ross, take a drink every time that:

·He stares at Hathaway across a crowded ER.

·He tries to see Hathaway off duty at an inappropriate time and gets rejected (if you're watching the new series, change this to 'each time he kisses Hathaway').

·A patient reminds Dr Ross of the importance of true love.

·He sleeps with Hathaway.

·He calls social services in to help with a patient.

·He says the word 'kiddo'.

·He ruffles any child's hair.

·He does something to jeopardise his career.

·He does something to save his career.

·His dad contacts him. He sees his dad.

·He can't keep a secret told to him in the strictest confidence.

If you picked Dr Benton, take a drink every time that:

·He clashes with other medical staff.

·He allows Carter to do a new procedure.

·He gets something wrong during a routine operation.

·He says something sarcastic.

·He goes on a date.

·He apologises to another member of staff for his arrogance.

·He muscles in on someone else's procedure.

·He says something kind to any ER member.

·He seems to actually care about a patient.

If you picked Nurse Hathaway, take a drink every time that:

·She looks at Dr Ross across a crowded ER.

·She is not wearing her usual pink scrubs.

·She goes out of her way to help a patient.

·She mentions the word 'clinic'.

·She quits.

·She goes out on a date with somebody other than Dr Ross.

If you picked Jeannie, take a drink every time that:

·Any nurse tells her, 'That's a PA job'.

·She tells any nurse, 'That's a nurse's job'.

·She mentions that she is married.

·Her ex-husband appears or is mentioned in a conversation.

·She talks to anyone about being HIV positive.

·She gets worried when she attempts an internal procedure.

·She gets fired.

·She sleeps with Dr Benton.

·She sleeps with anybody else from the ER.

If you picked Dr Weaver, take a drink every time that:

·Somebody knocks her cane away.

·She contradicts another doctor, quotes the regulations or mentions budgetary restraints.

·Someone makes fun of her.

·She has an argument with another doctor or a patient's family.

·She makes a 'recommendation' to Dr Greene.

·She goes out on a date with somebody.

·She complains.

If you picked Jerry, take a drink every time that:

·He appears on screen in a wildly coloured shirt.

·He corrects someone that he is the 'emergency services coordinator'.

·He appears in a costume of some sort.

·He is involved with something decidedly dodgy.

·He blows up an ambulance with a rocket launcher (quite specific this one, so drink your whole pint).

If you picked Dr Lewis, take a drink every time that:

·She gets in an argument with another doctor.

·She goes out on a date.

·Chloe appears.

·Chloe's boyfriend appears.

·Chloe reappears, with a new boyfriend.

·Chloe claims she'll take care of 'Little Susie'.

·Chloe smokes/drinks while talking about her baby.

·She kisses another ER doctor.

·Someone calls her 'Big Susie'.

·She brings 'Little Susie' into the ER.

If you picked Dr Del Amico, take a drink every time that:

·She and Dr Carter seem to get close.

·She rejects Dr Carter.

·She loses a patient.

·She complains about the size of her apartment.

·She flicks back her hair.

·She mentions her boyfriend (drink double if you actually get to see him).

If you picked Dr Cordet, take a drink every time that:

·She flirts with Dr Benton.

·She flirts with another member of the ER staff.

·She performs a new procedure.

·Someone mentions the fact that she's British.

·She mentions England, the NHS or her home.

·She kisses Dr Benton.

·Someone calls her 'Lizzie'.

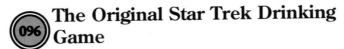

The Original Star Trek Drinking Game

Boldly go where no men have gone before with the Starship *Enterprise* and a crate of beer.

ESSENTIAL SUPPLIES

EPISODES OF THE ORIGINAL, KIRK-STARRING STAR TREK. BEER.

Please note: This entertainment is based upon the original *Star Trek* – the *Star Trek* with Kirk, Bones and Spock; the *Star Trek* where the engines "cannae take it, Captain"; the *Star Trek* where the guys in the red jumpers have a life expectancy of about ten minutes if they're chosen to accompany Kirk on a planetary mission. So, watch closely and take a sip from your drink if anything listed below happens onscreen:

- ·Kirk gets the girl.
- ·Kirk gets the alien girl.
- ·Kirk outwits a super computer.
- ·Kirk worries about violating the Prime Directive. Then violates it anyway.
- ·Kirk's shirt gets ripped in a fight.
- ·Kirk takes responsibility for the whole crew.
- ·Kirk says 'Phasers on stun'.

- ·Spock shows faint signs of emotion.
- ·Spock uses the Vulcan neck pinch.
- ·Spock gazes into his science computer and sees more than just a blue light.
- ·Spock says 'Illogical'.
- ·Spock says 'Fascinating'.
- ·Spock says 'Indeed'.
- ·Bones says 'He's dead, Jim'.

BOLLOXED FACTOR...

·Bones points out that, 'I'm a doctor, not a [insert job description here]'. For example a mechanic, gardener, etc.

·Scotty complains about the state of the warp engines and the speed requested by the Captain.

·Against all the odds, Scotty pulls off a technological feat that's never been done before. Usually with a cotton bud, some wire and a roll of sticky-back plastic.

·Chekov promotes Russian history.

·Chekov says 'But Keptin…'

·Sulu sets course or Sulu has the con.

·Uhura says, 'Hailing frequencies open'.

·Uhura opens a channel in all frequencies and all languages.

·A security guard in a red shirt dies on an alien planet.

·The away team's weapons are powerless against a new alien.

·The transporter system is inoperative.

·Dilithium crystals are drained, broken or missing.

·The shields are about to collapse.

·A newly discovered planet is 'much like Earth'.

The Raiders of the Lost Ark Drinking Game

097

An easy re-creation of a game played in the smash hit Indiana Jones movie.

ESSENTIAL SUPPLIES

SEVERAL BOTTLES OF HARSH VODKA. TEN SHOT GLASSES.

Remember the scene in *Raiders of the Lost Ark*? Picture the feisty Ms. Marian Ravenwood – she's the heroine, the one who owns the bar in Russia and wears the vital headpiece to the Staff of Ra around her neck. Before Indiana Jones arrives, Ms. Ravenwood competes in a drinking game with one of her more surly patrons.

It works like this: she stands ten shot glasses in two rows, one row of five glasses for each person. These glasses are then filled with the deadliest vodka she can find – this stuff can take paint off walls, it's a couple of degrees away from being an efficient jet fuel, etc. Once full, the two combatants drink one glass in turn, repeating the filling-up process until somebody falls on the floor in a drunken stupor. All you have to do is re-create this drinking experience, with shot glasses of your own and the meanest vodka you can find. Two people enter the game, but only one may leave slightly sober...

BOLLOXED FACTOR...

The Friends Drinking Game

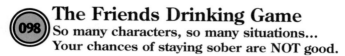

098 So many characters, so many situations...
Your chances of staying sober are NOT good.

ESSENTIAL SUPPLIES

A STACK OF FRIENDS EPISODES. BEER.

It's one of the most popular sit-coms in the world and so it's an easy target for drinking-games enthusiasts who have constructed this show-based drink-a-thon to combine heavy boozing with mellow, populist comedy.

And without further ado, here's how the game works. Just settle down in front of the TV, rip open that crate of lager, pop open a bottle and take a gulp whenever any of the actions listed below occur on the TV screen. So watch to see whether:

- Phoebe says, 'Duh!'
- Chandler waves his arms around in a wild manner while trying to say something important.
- Ross takes longer to say a sentence than a normal person would.
- Rachel calls someone 'Honey'.
- A celebrity guest makes an appearance.
- Any of the six characters drinks or mentions coffee.
- The exterior of Central Perk is shown.
- The exterior of Monica/Rachel's and Chandler/Joey's apartment building is shown.
- Any of the six are shown at their places of work.
- Any of the main character's parents show up.
- Any two or more main characters hug.
- Joey doesn't understand something that is obvious to everybody else.
- The hallway between Monica/Rachel's and Chandler/Joey's apartment is shown.
- Gunther shows just how much he loves Rachel.
- An animal is shown (Marcel the monkey, the duck, etc.).
- Ross and Rachel argue.

BOLLOXED FACTOR...

Now it starts to get interesting. Take two gulps if any of the following takes place:

·Phoebe plays a song on her guitar (add an extra gulp if it's 'Smelly Cat').
·The inside of Phoebe's apartment is shown.
·The inside of Ross' apartment is shown.
·All six main characters hang out in Monica/Rachel's apartment.
·Anyone makes a reference to an old TV show.
·Joey goes on a film/TV/theatre audition.
·Ross mentions Ben, Carol or Susan.
·Any of the six main characters kiss a non-main character.
·Ross gets jealous.
·Phoebe drives her grandma's taxi.
·Monica tidies up.
·Joey and Chandler buy a new piece of furniture.
·Joey and Chandler build a new piece of furniture.
·All six main characters play a game.

But to make it really exciting... drink triple the usual gulp if any of the stuff below happens:

·Joey actually understands the opposite sex.
·Marcel returns.
·Phoebe says something sensible.
·Monica dates a relatively normal person her own age. At least twice.
·Ben has a major speaking part in any episode.
·Phoebe's dad arrives.
·Dr Green is nice to Ross.
·Janice laughs.
·Janice says 'Oh. My. God…'
·Chandler drops his sarcastic, cynical facade.

The South Park Drinking Game

 099 A game where the words 'Oh my God, they killed Kenny!' can get you into BIG trouble.

ESSENTIAL SUPPLIES

A COLLECTION OF SOUTH PARK EPISODES. BEER.

Another adult 'toon, another set of simple rules to turn it into a drinking game. Line up a couple of episodes of *South Park*, get some mates round, set up the beers and drink down the booze whenever any of the following actions or events occur:

- Kenny dies.
- Rats carry off Kenny's head.
- Cartman says, 'Son of a bitch!'
- An animal is used in any sexual manner.
- Someone farts.
- Someone farts and it's on fire (drink twice).
- Chef sings.
- Chef makes up a nonsensical word.
- Mr. Hat swears.
- Kyle kicks the baby.
- The baby says: 'Don't kick the baby'.
- Someone says, 'Sweet!'
- Cartman says he's not fat, just big-boned.
- Mr Garrison explains his debased version of history.
- Kenny speaks.
- Jesus appears.
- Any Jewish reference is made.
- Kyle's mom is called a bitch.
- Anything explodes.
- Cartman is called a fatass.
- There is a non-fart-related reference to arses.

BOLLOXED FACTOR...

·The cows appear.

·Kyle says, '… make sweet love…'

·Cartman says: 'Kickass!'

·Stan gets the crap beaten out of him by his sister.

·Chef mentions love.

·Cartman says: "Beefcake!"

·The bus driver yells.

·Special guests appear.

·Chef swears.

·Chef refers to the boys as 'crackers'.

·Officer Barbrady tries to cover up an incident.

·Stan knows the moral of the story.

·Cartman mentions pie.

·The kids look at Terence and Phillip farting on each other.

·The genetic engineer wants to reform his mad scientist ways.

·The genetic engineer uses 'lusciously' when he speaks.

·Ned sings with his cancer kazoo.

·Real pictures are used as posters in the background.

·Someone other than Kenny dies.

The Reservoir Dogs Drinking Game

100 'Drunks to the left of me, drunks to the right, here I am, pissed in the middle with you...'

ESSENTIAL SUPPLIES

RESERVOIR DOGS THE MOVIE. BEER.

An easy game, with the easiest rules you'll ever come across. The key to drinking in The Reservoir Dogs Drinking Game is NOT to quaff, scull, imbibe and down whenever an action occurs on the screen (e.g. the botched heist, the ear-slicing scene, etc.), but simply to take a drink whenever any of the characters in the movie uses the word 'f*ck'. Our congratulations to any of you that manage to keep to this one-swig-per-f*ck rule and make it to the end of the movie with your sanity (and the majority of your brain cells) intact. If you don't, we won't think any less of you. Put it this way... have you any idea how many times the F-word is used in *Reservoir Dogs*? It's more than you think...

BOLLOXED FACTOR...

 Hints and Tips

You can, we're sure, think of other movies where the same game can be played. None is as good as this one...

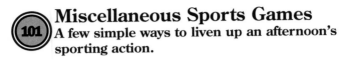

Miscellaneous Sports Games
101 A few simple ways to liven up an afternoon's sporting action.

ESSENTIAL SUPPLIES

CRICKET, FOOTBALL, TENPIN BOWLING, TENNIS, BASEBALL. FIND A SPORT AND SIMPLY ADD BEER.

There are very few games that exist to liven up an afternoon's sport. Until now that is. Because here, we've gathered together a collection of sports-based amusements that can liven up a football game, inject a little excitement into tennis and allow you to drink while watching Formula 1 grand prix racing.

The Soccer Drinking Game

This game allows you to drink and to enjoy a game of televised footy without having to constantly reference a list of actions and events. Here's how it works: played with two players, or with two equal teams, the basic idea is that each team must take a drink whenever the ball is in their side's half of the field, stopping when it passes over the half-way line to the opposing side's half.

The Formula 1 Drinking Game

There are many ways to take the fast-paced action of F1 and turn it into a drinking game too. Each drinker could adopt one of the teams, taking a sip for each time one of the team's cars completes a lap. Or, more seasoned drinkers may like to try the Pitstop variant, where players only drink during pitstops in the race, but must keep drinking for the length of time the car on camera is stationary in the pit lane.

The Tennis Drinking Game

Liven up a tennis match with The Tennis Drinking Game, an entertainment that seems to work best with the slowest type of tennis you can find – the women's game. While men's tennis is dominated by big- hitters and short rallies, women's tennis is perfect for changing into a drinking game. Try these rules out for size: best played

BOLLOXED FACTOR...

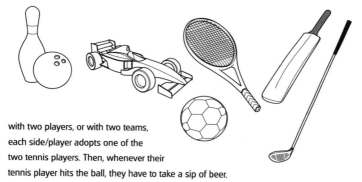

with two players, or with two teams,
each side/player adopts one of the
two tennis players. Then, whenever their
tennis player hits the ball, they have to take a sip of beer.
When the players sit down between games, that's the only time that you're allowed
to visit the toilet.

The Cricket Drinking Game

The Cricket Drinking Game is best played by a single player who wants to get well-
and-truly tanked on his/her own. The rules? One gulp per run, of course. Or maybe, one
drink (pint, half-pint or short) per man out. Or perhaps you could mutate a version of
the word game Buzz – when a team's score reaches a multiples of, say, 3, 5 and 7 (or
features any of those numbers in its score), then the players must drink a penalty. For
the baseball variation, drink whener there's a hit, strike, home run... you get the picture.

The Golf Drinking Game

Either drink one finger of beer per shot played or drink for the number of seconds a
player's ball flies through the air.

The Tenpin Bowling Drinking Game

There are ten pins standing at the bottom of the lane. A player comes up to bowl and
knocks down seven of the ten with his/her first ball. Take the seven downed pins away
from the original ten and that leaves three. Therefore the other players must drink three
fingers of beer.

7 BAR GAMES

If all you want is a game that requires no extras other than the pub or bar you're sat in, this is the section for you. Admittedly, for some of these games you'll need specialised equipment but, as most modern pubs are starting to carry pub games (like chess, draughts, kerplunk, etc.) to keep their drinkers happy, finding the props specified shouldn't be too much of a problem. Of course, the clutter-free drinking games remain the most challenging and daring of all guzzling entertainments. So pick a pub and settle down.

The Pub Crawl

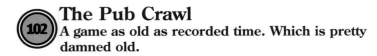

102 A game as old as recorded time. Which is pretty damned old.

ESSENTIAL SUPPLIES

A LARGE AMOUNT OF PUBS, IN A VERY SMALL AREA. MONEY.

Now come on. You know how this game works. You start off in a pub, drink one glass of lager (or a half-pint) and then move on to the next pub in the street, where you repeat the drinking ritual. Then you move onto the next pub, the next, and so on, until (a) you can't drink another drop, (b) the pubs shut or (c) you fall over and spend the night in the gutter next to a small cat nibbling at a three-day-old pork ball. It's a game enjoyed by thousands across the country, a game that works particularly well in towns with an obscene number of watering holes in close proximity to each other.

Variants: The Three-Legged Pub Crawl: As in the traditional Pub Crawl, players move from pub to pub, drinking down an agreed measure of alcohol and moving on. The Three-Legged Pub Crawl gives the usual game an old playground twist. Simply stand two willing drunkards together, tie the right leg of one to the left leg of the other (creating 'three' legs) and set them out on the pub crawl as before. If you have trouble controlling your own legs after eight pints of Kronenbourg, imagine how tough it is to keep somebody else standing up...

Pub Golf: Pub Golf takes the basic rules of the traditional Pub Crawl and forces a golfing theme on to it. Here's how it works: organise your players into pairs as if you were going to play the Three-Legged Pub Crawl variant. One player of the two will be the 'Professional' player, which means that he/she will have to drink pints as the pair moves from pub to pub.

BOLLOXED FACTOR...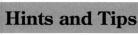

Hints and Tips

Sensible people will make sure that everyone meets up beforehand and gets something decent to eat before piling on the booze.

The second player in the pair, will be known as the 'Amateur' player, which in turn means that he/she will have to drink half-pints or shorts in every pub the pair visits. Like playing a round of golf, the teams must visit nine holes (pubs), each one of which has a Par 3 rating. What this means is that each player in the pair must down their drink in three gulps or less. The scores are combined so that if one player finishes his/her drink in 4 gulps, the other has only 2 gulps left (i.e. 3 + 3 = 6; 4 + 2 = 6) to finish his/her drink to get a par for the hole. However, if the pro player downs his/her drink in one go, this is considered a hole-in-one and both players can move onto the next hole. Shots are dropped going to the toilet (one shot), spilling your drink (one shot) or falling over (two shots). The team with the highest overall score at the end of the nine-pub crawl loses the game and must drink a forfeit decided by the other participating players..

The Broom-Handle Game
Another simple game with a surprisingly high humour factor.

ESSENTIAL SUPPLIES

A BEER GARDEN. BEER. A BROOM HANDLE.

Gather together a large group of friends and give everybody a pint of something strong and lager-like. The idea behind the game is simple – one at a time, the players drink half of their pint and run up the beer garden to a broom handle laying on the grass. The participating player then picks up the sweeping stick, puts the brush on the turf and holds the handle up vertically like a pole. Quickly, the player then places his forehead on the end of the vertically standing broom handle and runs around it ten times. After the tenth rotation, all the player then has to do is run or walk back up the garden to drink the rest of his/her pint. Dizziness, however, should take control at this point, and the drunken player should hilariously cartwheel into the fence/flowerbed/tables, etc. The winner is the one who makes it back to their pint and drinks it. Losers get laughed at.

BOLLOXED FACTOR...

Hints and Tips

Take a tip from ice figure-skaters and keep an eye on a fixed point as you twirl around. This is meant to help.

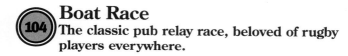

Boat Race
104 The classic pub relay race, beloved of rugby players everywhere.

ESSENTIAL SUPPLIES

TWO TEAMS. BEER. CLOTHES YOU DON'T MIND GETTING WET.

Divide a group of wannabe drinkers into two equal teams. Give each member of the team a pint of the 'amber nectar' and line them up in an organised row, one behind the other. The idea of the Boat Race is ludicrously simple – it's a trumped-up relay race, but with beer. When somebody shouts go (or drops a handkerchief, fires a gun, taps a table, whatever...) the team member at the head of the line starts drinking their pint as fast as they possibly can. When they've finished, they must quickly raise their empty glass and place it, upside down, on top of their head. This movement then signals the player behind to start draining the foamy contents of their pint, and again when the player finishes, their glass must be placed upside down on top of their head. Play continues in this fashion until all of the players in the line have finished their drinks and have upturned pint glasses on their heads. The first team to finish all of their drinks and place all of their glasses in this position wins the race. The losers then have to face a suitable drinking penalty...

BOLLOXED FACTOR...

  # Hints and Tips

Don't plan on moving on to any posh locations after playing this – you and your clothes will absolutely stink of beer.

Jengaholic

105 **A game that requires a high drinking stamina and steady hands.**

ESSENTIAL SUPPLIES

A BOX OF JENGA BLOCKS. BEER.

Now that more pubs and bars have games behind the bar, Jengaholic is just one of the many booze-related variants you can play. The idea is an easy one (although for this game, you're better off using your own Jenga set).

Before you build up your Jenga tower, painstakingly label each wooden block with some sort of action or drinking penalty, e.g. 'Take off an item of clothing', 'Drink three sips of beer', "Tell a player to drink three sips', and so on. Then, quite obviously, when a player removes a block he/she must perform the action written on it. Failure to do so incurs a hefty drinking penalty, as does knocking the Jenga tower over. The primary rule is to drink and to keep drinking. Any other rules you make are purely to spice up the proceedings.

BOLLOXED FACTOR...

 Hints and Tips

Keep a bar towel on hand for wiping up any spillages. There's nothing worse than trying to play Jenga with wet fingers.

Ker-Drunk
A perversion of the classic kids' game, now with much higher stakes.

(106)

ESSENTIAL SUPPLIES

A GAME OF KERPLUNK. A JUG. BEER.

Like Jengaholic, Ker-Drunk is another game that takes a traditional gaming favourite and gives it a drink-related twist. It can be played in two ways.

Number 1: Fill a jug with beer and play Kerplunk as usual. Whoever removes the plastic straw that makes all the marbles drop into the bottom has to drink the contents of the jug.

Number 2: Is slightly more deadly... Players take it in turns to pull out a straw from the Kerplunk tower. This time, however, every time a marble drops, the player responsible must add some of his drink (whatever that may be) to the empty jug. This process continues until a lethal concoction of drink froths in the jug and some unlucky soul pulls out the straw that makes the remaining marbles cascade into the bottom of the tower. When this happens, the unfortunate player must drink down the jug's contents. He/she may not want to play another game after doing so.

BOLLOXED FACTOR...

 Hints and Tips

If you're playing version 2, be sure and choose drinks that don't mix well. Like Bailey's, lager and white wine.

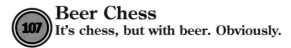

Beer Chess
107 It's chess, but with beer. Obviously.

ESSENTIAL SUPPLIES

AN OVERSIZED CHESSBOARD (FAILING THIS, SOME BATHROOM TILES). CANS OF BEER.

Beer Chess is played using beer as the pieces. And because the pieces are cans or bottles, you're going to require a slightly larger chessboard than usual. If you can't find one, get a collection of white and black bathroom tiles. For a more portable, pub-based board, try different coloured beer coasters. For the pieces, one player should use bottles, the other cans.

A typical set-up might look like this: White would play with eight pawns (bottles of Becks); two rooks (bottles of Heineken); two bishops (bottles of Miller Lite); two knights (bottles of Kronenbourg); a King (bottle of Budweiser)and a Queen (bottle of Grolsch). Black would play with cans – eight pawns (cans of Carling); two rooks (cans of Fosters); two bishops (cans of Grolsch); two knights (cans of Heineken); a King (can of Budweiser); and a Queen (can of Special Brew). It might help to label the cans so you don't forget which is which.

The rules for the game are: (1) when a player moves a piece on the board, he/she must take a sip from the piece moved. (2) When a piece is captured by the opposing player, the owner of the captured piece must drink the contents of the can/bottle taken. (3) The 'Castling' manoeuvre costs two sips from each piece to complete. (4) The Pawn move 'En Passant' costs one sip. (5) If a pawn reaches the eighth rank on the board, the player can exchange it for a queen – the opposing player must drink the entire contents of the exchanged pawn. (6) Once a piece has been sipped, the piece MUST be moved. (7) When a player is put in 'check', the checked player must take a sip from the King piece. (8) When one player is checkmated, the losing player must drink the contents of his remaining pieces.

BOLLOXED FACTOR...

Hints and Tips

Never play this game with anyone you know to be from Russia. They can all play chess like Spassky and drink like Boris Yeltsin.

Booze Draughts

108 It's draughts, but with vodka, gin, rum and other popular spirits.

ESSENTIAL SUPPLIES

A CHESSBOARD. SPIRITS. SHOT GLASSES.

All the fun of Beer Chess but without the complicated rules, Booze Draughts simply replaces the red and black pieces of the traditional game with shot glasses filled with spirits. To distinguish between the two players, one should drink a colourless spirit (say, vodka, gin, schnapps, etc.) while the other should plump for a coloured drink (whisky, rum, etc.)

Set your glasses out in the usual draughts way and then play the game as usual. This time, however, when a piece is captured by the opposing player, the player who owns the captured piece must down the glass. Play continues until somebody either (a) wins, or (b) falls over.

BOLLOXED FACTOR...

Hints and Tips

Try not to let yourself get set up for one of those lethal multiple takes. It could be the end of you.

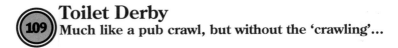

Toilet Derby
109 Much like a pub crawl, but without the 'crawling'...

ESSENTIAL SUPPLIES

PUBS. WOMEN'S/GENTS' TOILETS. BEER.

A ludicrous game best played when you've either (a) had far too much to drink and you don't care, or (b) had very little to drink and you can still run without throwing up. The rules are as follows. (Men) pick five pubs in close proximity to each other and, in race conditions, run into each one, hurtle into the Women's toilets, touch the back wall and leave as fast as your legs will carry you. Repeat this process in the next four pubs; the last man to finish drinks a hefty forfeit. (Women) pick five pubs in close proximity to each other and, in race conditions, run into each one, hurtle into the Men's toilets, touch the back wall and leave as fast as your legs will carry you. Repeat this process in the next four pubs; the last woman to finish drinks a hefty forfeit.

Variant: Bog Crush: A game that only works when you have a large group of people and a suitably crammed toilet cubicle. The idea is a simple one. Cram yourselves into the cubicle one by one. The last person to fit into the space, or the person(s) who can't squeeze themselves in must drink the alco-forfeit. (Note: a much cleaner variant of this is the phone-box game.)

BOLLOXED FACTOR...

 Hints and Tips

You're much better off playing this in an area where nobody knows you or your friends. You won't be tracked down then.

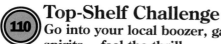

Top-Shelf Challenge

110 Go into your local boozer, gaze at the top-shelf spirits... feel the thrill.

ESSENTIAL SUPPLIES

A PUB. A WELL-STOCKED BAR. SPIRITS. LOTS OF CASH.

Simply wander into any pub (as long as the pub chosen has a large spirits supply) and stand determinedly at the bar. Then, from right to left (or vice versa), order a shot of every spirit on the top shelf behind the bar. This should deliver an awesome mix of rums, whiskies, vodkas and gins, each one of which must be downed in quick succession. The winner is the one who makes it to the end of their row first. (Also known as The Optics Challenge.)

Variants: The Bartop Challenge: The Bartop Challenge raises the stakes, daring you to drink the lesser-known alcohols that most people have with lemonade, coke or soda. This means drinks like Blue Curacao, Archers Peach Schnapps and so on, plus the less-than-palatable collection of cordials (which should be imbibed neat) such as blackcurrant, lime, etc. Again, work your way from right to left (or vice versa), the winner is the one who finishes his/her assembled drinkage first. If you're feeling kind, you can allow mixers to be used.

The Beer Pump Challenge: Also known as the Lager Challenge. Starting at the end of the bar that's home to the coke and lemonade gun, simply book your ticket to alco-oblivion by having a pint of each beer or lager that is available on draught. As usual, the winner is the one who can finish the line of pumps first. Players may NOT want to line up the beers, but slowly work their way along the bartop pumps as an evening progresses. Then again, you might not.

BOLLOXED FACTOR...

Hints and Tips

This is a game best played in the company of somebody who's just won a fortune at the bookies, and is prepared to pay for everything.

Snakes & Ladders
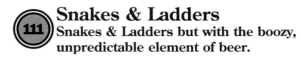

111 Snakes & Ladders but with the boozy, unpredictable element of beer.

ESSENTIAL SUPPLIES

A SNAKES & LADDERS BOARD. A SIX-SIDED DIE. SOME COINS. BEER.

Gather a group of friends (up to six can play) and determine which one of you will go first by rolling a single die. Whoever gets the highest roll starts first (if two players tie, these players roll again, highest roll wins). The aim of the game is to get to the top before anybody else. Participating players place their tokens (here, read coins – make sure you have plenty of different ones) on the starting square and roll the die to see how many squares they move.

Here's where the beer comes in: (1) if a player's token lands at the bottom of a ladder, the lucky player can move it to the top of the ladder and the other players must drink a sip (or two sips) per level that the ladder climbs up. (2) Likewise, if the player's token lands on the head of a snake, the unfortunate player must move his token down to the bottom, consuming one or more sips of beer per level descended. (3) If a player's token lands atop another's at the end of their go, both players involved must take a drink from their beers (again, one sip or two). (4) On every Snakes & Ladders board there is one immensely-long, game-winning ladder, and one terrifyingly lengthy, game-hindering snake. If a player should be fortunate enough to land on the immensely-long ladder, all of the other players in the game must 'shotgun' a beer in his/her honour. If, however, a player should land on the terrifyingly lengthy snake, this unfortunate soul must shotgun a beer himself, from a can pierced once each by the other players. Note: the immensely long ladder and the terrifyingly lengthy snake don't have to be a cue for shotgunning, inventive players may want to assign a different rule to these two bogey squares, e.g. Tequila

BOLLOXED FACTOR...

 Hints and Tips

You must resist the temptation, once pissed, to try and play the game with real snakes and real ladders. No matter how much fun it sounds.

slammers, enforced nudity, flaming Drambuie, and so on.

The game ends when one player rolls the exact number needed to reach square 100, the winner's square. Anybody who tries to enter the square and fails by rolling over the amount needed must drink a gulp of beer per point. For example, if a player sits on square 97 and rolls a six trying to end the game, they overshoot by three (97 + 6 = 103) and so must neck down three gulps of beer as a penalty. When a player finally reaches the winning square, the rest of the players must drink a swig of beer for every level that they are 'below' the winner, e.g. a player on square 64 is three levels below the top rung and so must quaff three swigs of beer. Lastly, if any dice leave the table during a role, saddle the offending player with a two-gulp fine.

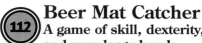

Beer Mat Catcher
A game of skill, dexterity, hand/eye coordination and very large hands.

ESSENTIAL SUPPLIES

A PUB. SOME BEER MATS. A TABLE. BEER.

Simple, yet effective; annoy the other patrons in the bar by stealing their beer mats and piling the cardboard squares together in the middle of the table. Then, one by one, the players shuffle up to the table, and place a beer mat on the lip so that half rests on the table and half hangs over the edge.

Then, in one flowing motion, the idea is to flip the beer mat up with your outstretched fingers (palm down) and to catch it with the same hand. Failure incurs a one-gulp penalty. When all of the participating players have done this, the stakes are raised to two mats. One mat is placed atop the other and the player attempts to flip and catch the tiny pile as before.

When all players have done this, the level of mats increases to three, then four, five, six and so on until a weighty mass of beer mats dares each player to flip and catch it. To clarify those rules again:

(1) The player must flip and catch the pile of mats with the same hand; (2) the player must catch all of the mats in the pile. Even if one slips out, the player's go is deemed a failure and he/she must drink.

BOLLOXED FACTOR...

 Hints and Tips

Unlikely as it may seem, water can once again be your friend. Wet beer mats tend to stick together better than dry ones, you see...

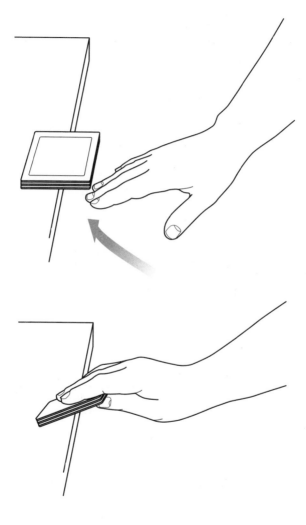

APPENDIX

APPENDIX I: BAR PHILOSOPHY

'Well Bob, you should think yourself fortunate that you still have your liver INSIDE you. My liver and I parted company about a year ago. I can get up in the morning after a heavy night, go down stairs and see my liver sitting there in the kitchen with a big fried breakfast, a cigarette and a haggard look. Usually, we end up sitting on the couch staring at mindnumbing morning TV. Because neither of us can be bothered to get up and find the remote control...'

'Rehab? Oh yeah right, that's a great game. I'm stuck on Level 7. Isn't that the one with the Undead Flesh-Ripping Tequila-Slamming Mother Superiors of Oblivion? I can beat them, but I'll be damned if I can get past the flying wheelbarrows with the rocket launchers.'

'Concerned of Chipping Sodbury says: "What most people tend not to realise is that beer is a 'gateway drug'". By this I mean that anybody who drinks beer on a regular basis, stands a greater risk of becoming involved with more dangerous drugs and narcotics – heroin, crack, mescaline, valium, the list is almost endless. So stop the madness. Protect yourself by drinking so much that you won't have time for any other drugs.'

'Is drinking beer better than sex? Of course it isn't. How can you compare the two? That's like saying that lime cordial is better than sniffing. Of course there's no reason why you can't combine beer and sex for the ultimate experience. Sadly the same doesn't go for sniffing and lime cordial.'

'Will continued consumption of alcoholic milk eventually give kids the milk-shakes?'

'If ever there was a piece of hard evidence that alcohol can make you see clearer, it is this handy tip that appeared in an American newspaper. "Another way to wipe your eyeglasses free of streaks is put a drop of vodka on each lens." Unfortunately, there is no mention of how you go about removing the subsequent lick marks from them.'

'We drunkards hold the future in our hands... so try not to spill beer all over it.'

'Yesterday, scientists in the United States revealed that beer contains small traces of female hormones. To prove their theory, they conducted an experiment where they fed 100 men 12 pints of beer and observed that 100% of them started talking nonsense and couldn't drive.'

'If a hand falls on a piano key, but no one around is sober, does it still make a sound?'

'Steve looked concerned: "Won't your wife hit the ceiling if you come home at three o'clock in the morning, pissed out of your face?" Dave merely shrugged. "Of course she will, she's a terrible shot!"'

'See life as it really is. View it through the bottom of an empty brown bottle.'

'No buddy, I've never tried to get my cat drunk. I am totally against giving animals alcohol, and I'm even more against blowing smoke at them. However, what my cat does in his own time is his own business.'

'Yeah, my wife's angry with me again. Just because I woke up last night, got out of bed and pissed in the laundry basket. I mean, is that fair? The cat does it too!'

APPENDIX II: GREAT BEER QUOTES

Graffiti spotted in a pub toilet: 'You don't buy the drink here, you only rent it.'
Anon.

'Man, being reasonable, must get drunk; The best of life is but intoxication.' George Gordon Byron (*Don Juan*)

'Drinking when we are not thirsty and making love all year round, madam; that is all there is to distinguish us from other animals.' *Pierre Beaumarchais (The Barber of Seville)*

'Work is the curse of the drinking classes.' Oscar Wilde.

'I may be drunk, but you are ugly, and in the morning I shall be sober, but you will still be ugly.' Sir Winston Churchill

'Sir, if you were my husband, I would poison your drink.' Lady Astor to Winston Churchill. 'Madam, if you were my wife, I would drink it.' Sir Winston Churchill's reply.

'Reality is an illusion that occurs due to the lack of alcohol.' Anon.

'When I read about the evils of drinking, I gave up reading.' Henry Youngman

'Twenty-four hours in a day, twenty-four beers in a case. Coincidence?' Anon.

'I'd rather have a bottle in front of me, than a frontal lobotomy.' Tom Waits

'I never drink anything stronger than gin before breakfast. A woman drove me to drink and I didn't even have the decency to thank her. What contemptible scoundrel has stolen the cork to my lunch?' **WC Fields**

'The problem with the world is that everyone is a few drinks behind.' Humphrey Bogart

'You can't be a real country unless you have a beer and an airline; it helps if you have some kind of a football team, or some nuclear weapons, but at the very least you need a beer.' Frank Zappa

'Always do sober what you said you'd do drunk. That will teach you to keep your mouth shut.' Ernest Hemingway

'Men are like wine – some turn to vinegar, but the best improve with age.'
Pope John XXIII

**'Beer is proof that God loves us and wants us to be happy.'
Benjamin Franklin**

'I would kill everyone in this room for a drop of sweet beer.' Homer Simpson

**'You're not drunk if you can lie on the floor without holding on.'
Dean Martin**

'The only way to get rid of a temptation is to yield to it.' Oscar Wilde

APPENDIX III: ARE YOU DRINKING TOO MUCH?
A SELF-HELP GUIDE

Well, are you? And how do you know? Take this small self-help test and find out for certain. All you have to do is work your way through the following 15 questions – if you answer 'yes' to any of them, note the number of points that the question is worth. When you get to the bottom, total up the points that you've amassed and write down your final score. This will be transformed into the Drunk-O-Meter at the end. Here are those all-important questions:

1. **Do you ever lose arguments with inanimate objects? (1 point)**

2. **Do you ever have to hold on to the lawn to keep from falling off the Earth? (2 points)**

3. **Do you keep hitting the back of your head on the toilet seat? (1 point)**

4. **Do you ever or have you ever believed that alcohol is a major food group? (5 points)**

5. **Can you focus better with one eye closed? (1 point)**

6. **Has the car park ever moved somewhere completely different while you were in the pub? (2 points)**

7. **Have you ever fallen off the floor? (2 points)**

8. **Do you have twin sons and do you wonder why you named them Barley and Hops? (10 points)**

9. **Are you fond of 'liquid' lunches? (2 points)**

10. **When at an Alcoholic's Anonymous meeting, have you ever begun by saying: 'Hi, my name is... um...'? (5 points)**

11. **Do all of the patrons in your local pub say 'Hi' when you come in? (2 points)**

12. Do you have your own tankard or stool? (5 points)

13. Are you starting to find next-door's cat more and more attractive? (2 points)

14. Is next door's cat starting to find you more and more attractive? (2 points)

15. Do you recognise your wife when you DON'T see her through the bottom of a glass? (2 points)

HOW DID YOU SCORE?

1–10 POINTS: You're only a casual drinker, so you've got nothing to worry about.

10–20 POINTS: Whoah there, fella! You're hitting the booze fairly hard. If your symptoms persist, and they're combined with memory loss, you'd better start cutting down. If you can remember...

20–30 POINTS: It's surprising you can focus on this page long enough to read the questions. That you actually understood them was a bonus.

30+ POINTS: And you're still alive? Have you ever considered donating your body to medical science?

APPENDIX IV: 100 SIGNS THAT YOU ARE A DRUNKEN SOD

1. You have a top 10 beer list.
2. You grow a beard because it stops beer running down your chin.
3. Your heroes are George Best, Mickey Rourke and Jimmy Greaves.
4. Tequila worms fear you.
5. You fall down the stairs and don't spill any of your beer.
6. You never have a hangover... because you're always drunk.
7. You wake up to the sound of your dog drinking out of the toilet, and your throat is so dry that you join it for a quick swig.
8. You wake up to the sound of your dog drinking out of the toilet, but you don't have a dog.
9. Your only goal in life is to drink a six-pack of beer every day.
10. Half of your home decorations are empty beer bottles.
11. There IS photographic evidence.
12. You take communion and go back for more.
13. You're on your third liver transplant operation.
14. You have a notch on your belt for every pub you've been to.
15. You think drinking low-alcohol lager is like making love to a woman in a boat... it's too close to water.
16. You kiss/lick your girlfriend's neck in search of any spilt beer.
17. Every girl you look at looks like Cindy Crawford.
18. You think that something is wrong when the room stops spinning.
19. You can burp the entire alphabet forwards and backwards, and follow it with a recognisable rendition of 'Swing Low, Sweet Chariot'.
20. When you wake up in the morning your hair hurts and you think that someone has laid a shagpile carpet on your tongue.
21. You're on first-name terms at the rehab centre.
22. You have more furniture than you can remember after a night on the town.
23. You often urinate outdoors.
24. Somebody HAS laid a shagpile carpet on your tongue.
25. You try to brush something off your shoulder but it turns out to be the floor.
26. You think that beer ads make clear sense.
27. You think that beer ads are funny.
28. When you step into the shower in the morning, nothing happens for five minutes because the water is being absorbed into your dehydrated skin.
29. You spend nights sending ridiculous messages to people on the internet,

ending with, 'By the way, what are you drinking?'

30. You hope that your next girlfriend is the daughter of the bloke that owns the off-licence.

31. You ask out the daughter of the bloke who owns the off-licence. Even though she is only eight.

32. Your wife asks who you went out with last night and you say Jack Daniel's and Jim Beam.

33. The only reason that you cuddle up to your wife is because she's still got some beer left.

34. You are so dehydrated from last night's outlandish drinking binge that your genitals have shrunk into your body and you can't see them.

35. You wake up in the morning after a house party and drink down a few of the half-empty bottles left sitting around the room.

36. You wake up in the morning after a house party and drink down a few of the half-empty bottles left sitting around the room. Even the ones with ash floating in them.

37. You find yourself muttering: 'Honestly occifer I only had tree bears tonight!'

38. You need to take witnesses with you to confession because you can't quite remember what you've done and the vicar wouldn't believe you anyway.

39. The only workout you get over the weekend is the trip to the fridge and the trip to the bog.

40. You wake up, open your eyes and say: 'Shit, did I shag that?!'

41. You mix cocktails by the litre.

42. The off-licence has your beer ready before you even come in.

43. Beer companies give air miles and you can get a return to Australia after one night out.

44. Your friends call you at midday to ask if you want to go out drinking in the evening, but you have to say 'no' because you're already pissed.

45. You pour Irish Cream on your corn flakes instead of milk.

46. Your life savings are hidden in an empty beer can.

47. Your life savings are hidden in a half-full beer can.

48. You wake up with yellow rice up your nose, brown smudges on your shirt and a new set of ethnic dip-holders.

49. Every pub and off-licence in town sends you a Christmas card.

50. You're on first-name terms with every barman/barmaid in town.

51. You have your own reserved parking space outside the off-licence.
52. You fall asleep on the toilet.
53. You fall asleep before you make it to the toilet.
54. You use a cash machine (and get a receipt) more than ten times, so you have enough paper to go for a dump in the woods.
55. You go to bed with Cindy Crawford but wake up with Richard Gere.
56. You spend more than ten minutes reading or writing a web page about beer and spirits.
57. Your typical breakfast is cold pizza washed down with beer.
58. People say, 'You're drunk!' And you say, 'No I'm not'.
59. You stick your fingers down your throat to puke up so you can drink longer.
60. Your patio furniture consists of a park bench and a No Entry sign.
61. Your bath towels are small, brightly coloured and have FOSTERS written on them.
62. You need to shut one eye to see double.
63. You send your liver out to get dry-cleaned.
64. You say, 'yes, so drinking kills brain cells, but it only kills the weak ones'.
65. It takes two weeks to put the fire out after your cremation.
66. You take brewery tours more often than you visit your relatives.
67. Anything anyone says immediately becomes a drinking euphemism.
68. Your organ donor recipient wakes up with a hangover.
69. You know how to mix more drinks than the barman.
70. Too many children come up to you on the street and call you 'Daddy!'
71. Your friends call you 'the alcoholic' and you don't care.
72. Your toilet has a customised chin rest and handles.
73. You kick your girlfriend out of bed in order to sleep with your wastebasket.
74. You host a party and pass out several hours before the end.
75. The keg you buy says 20 standard drinks but you get five out of it.
76. You believe that spilling a beer is alcohol abuse.
77. You have a list of reasons why a beer is better than a woman.
78. You regularly wake to the greeting, 'Guess what YOU did last night!'
79. You go to the toilet to vomit, but you take your beer with you.
80. Your ideal woman is the one that can outdrink you.
81. You think of beer during masturbation.
82. You take your cat to bed and put your wife out for the night.
83. Your local pub goes bankrupt when you go on holiday for two weeks.
84. You spend 20 minutes trying unsuccessfully to start your car, only to realise it's not your car you're sitting in.

85. Your bar tab is greater than your monthly wage.
86. You think it was a bad night because you CAN remember where you were.
87. You don't want to have sex with your girlfriend because it cuts down on your drinking time.
88. You are always the last person up and drinking at the party.
89. You feel you have to stop drinking at least once a month, so you can go to bed sober, and wake up feeling so healthy and refreshed that you could be drinking twice as much as you did before.
90. You wake up in the middle of the night to take a piss and the next morning you awake to find yourself in bed with your best friend's parents.
91. You do something to a bouncer, he turns around ready to smack your head in, but sees it's you and then laughs and walks off shaking his head.
92. You take an hour to walk the 500 metres home.
93. You regularly take the ferry from Dover to Calais just to buy duty-free beer.
94. You can distinguish brands of beer just by the smell.
95. You would rather piss yourself than give up your barstool.
96. You puke in your mouth and swallow it while chatting up a girl, pretending that nothing has happened.
97. You stop brushing your teeth in the morning because the toothpaste clashes with the taste of your beer.
99. You hadn't noticed that we'd missed number 98.
100. You're dribbling more than your baby.

APPENDIX V: THE TOP 5 HANGOVER CURES

(1) Don't ever drink. Not even a little bit. This will guarantee that you never have to endure the horror of a hangover.

(2) If Tip 1 sounds just a bit too harsh, try Tip 2 – never drink enough to get screaming drunk. Limit yourself to one drink (maybe two) per week.

(3) Let's face it. Tips 1 and 2 are for wimps. If you are a regular drinker, try the tried and trusted Tip 3 – take a couple of asprin before you go to bed and drink at least two pints of water.

(4) If you can't stop drinking, there are some extra preventative measures you can try. It may help to know just what causes a hangover in the first place. For starters, a hangover is your body's way of telling you that you're dehydrated – the beer has caused some of the body's supply of water to evaporate. Secondly, the body is trying to cope with the effects of nervous shock – your system is hypersensitive, recovering from the ravages of the alcohol (which is a drug and mild depressant). Thirdly, you'll be suffering from a form of slight malnutrition – the alcohol has washed away some of the body's stored nutrients. To recuperate, follow the rehydration steps mentioned in Tip 3, and try to eat something sensible to restore the nutrients and vitamins that your body has lost. While a slap-up greasy fry-up is often regarded as a natural cure-all, fruit and vegetables should be ingested to boost your internal system.

(5) Ok. So you can't stop drinking. So what can you do? Well, if you're determined to drink like a fish, try NOT to: mix your drinks; drink a dizzying cocktail of coloured spirits (whiskey, rum, etc.); drink cheap red wine; drink trendy alcoholic mixes with sugary content.

APPENDIX VI: EVEN MORE CURES

Drink Sprite (to replace sugar) and take some asprin.

Have a packet of crisps, a litre of orange juice, a Mars bar, and a bottle of Lucozade.

Recover the old-fashioned way – throw up.

A pint glass filled with two-thirds tomato juice, one-third beer.

A can (or two) of coke, two non-drowsy Sinutabs and a slice of toast. Something with a lot of salt.

In a sherry glass, mix: one raw egg, one tablespoon of Worcestershire sauce, one soupspoon of red pepper sauce. Drink it in one.

As alcohol dehydrates your system, drink a lot of fruit juices (for the minerals) and do some exercise to sweat the rest of the alcohol out.

APPENDIX VII: DRINKING LEGENDS

As old as time itself, beer – the foundation of civilization – has a history that starts in the ancient world and evolves through many types and forms before it reaches the froth-headed pint that you can buy down the local today. Do religion and beer mix? Why did pubs once open at strange hours? Who invented Guinness? The answers to these legendary posers is revealed below...

THE ENGLISH PUB
The idea of the English 'pub' or 'public house' can be traced right back to the rudimentary ale houses and taverns that sprung up during the medieval era – the earliest drinking establishments were literally extensions of the brewers' homes, i.e. they were the 'public' part of the house. The origins of the famous pub signs and pub names are also rooted deep in history. Typically, as the working classes in early England often had no grasp of reading or writing, taverns and inns chose to advertise their presence using pictorial methods. In many cases, landlords plumped for instantly recognisable family crests (leading to pubs like The Red Lion or The Dragon); while others were inspired by traditional folklore (The Green Man is named after a mythical pagan who would cover himself in leaves) or their unquestioning devotion to the monarchy (The King's Head). Additional sources of ancient motivation included reflecting religion in a pub's sign (The Mitre, The Cross Keys); or naming the pub after a local profession or trade (The Baker's Arms). Nowadays, while you still find pubs that nod reverentially to the royals (The Prince Of Wales, The Windsor Castle), most modern pubs are more likely to be named after sports (football, cricket, etc.), famous people or as part of a themed, drinker-friendly chain.

DAVID LLOYD GEORGE
While not a renowned drinker (he was an ardent teetotaller), David Lloyd George was the man responsible for some of the UK's more bizarre drinking legislation. The story goes: in 1915, believing that the consumption of alcohol was damaging the war effort, he pushed through the controversial Defence of the Realm Act which stipulated that pubs were only allowed to open their doors to drinkers at lunchtime and in the evening. Until the late 1980s, these restricted opening hours remained in place, although public pressure has since repealed the law and English pubs, like their Irish counterparts, are permitted to open all day between the hours of 11am and 11pm. – sometimes even later!

TOBY PHILLPOT

A legendary ale drinker of considerable largesse whose caricatured likeness is immortalised on Toby jugs throughout the land. Think of him as the Oliver Reed of the nineteenth century.

ORIGINS

Beer is as old as history itself, its use – as a refreshing, 'safe' alternative to impure water – dates back to Roman Britain, ancient Egypt and beyond. And while early civilisations struggled to preserve fruit and meats, grain grown in the fields was the easiest foodstuff to store. Little surprise, then, that the versatile foodstuff became the basis for beers and ales, a cheap, easily produced drink that appealed to both rich and poor alike. According to some historians, the discovery of beer and brewing (and, obviously, bread) could be responsible for the end of mankind's nomadic lifestyle and his adoption of a static settlement where crops could be grown – thus beer leads to feudalism, crop rotation, the industrial revolution, computers and so on. And although the first beers were little more than soaked grain, they were widely popular – beer, for example, was often paid to workers in the ancient world instead of cash. Egypt is largely credited as the birthplace of brewing, and its citizens advanced the technique by first 'malting' the grain (leaving it out in the sun to dry, thus releasing the starch and sugar, before mashing it and leaving it to ferment). Food and beer were later combined in 'beer bread', surely the ultimate nutritional combination.

Despite the fact that Egypt's brewing industry was destroyed by a Muslim invasion of the country in the ninth century, beer-making knowledge had spread far and wide through the Old World – probably by ship to the fringes of what would become Eastern Europe, into Germany, France, Spain, the British Isles and Scandinavia. Only Italy and the more southern countries where grapes were abundant and the weather was warm, stayed with wine-producing – although after they conquered Britain, the invading Romans eventually turned to brewing when supplies of their favourite plonk ran out. And while the early Brits also made alcoholic drinks from apples (cider) and honey (mead), beer quickly became the most popular beverage. In early Europe, beer was brewed at home by women. People would often go to the home of the woman who brewed the best beer to sample it for themselves, giving rise to the 'public house' or, as we now know it, the 'pub'.

MONKS

While most early beer-brewing was confined to the home, the Christian Church was quick to see the potential of the popular drink and jumped into the production of their own booze with extraordinary zeal. From the eleventh century, monasteries throughout Europe became mini-breweries – not only was the beer that was produced sold to travellers, but it became a basic part of the monks' meagre, unspectacular diet. History records that two or more brews were often made from a single malted-grain mash; the first would be a full-strength beverage, a beer of high quality reserved for the abbot, the archbishop and possibly the nobles that lived nearby; while the second (and possibly third) was much weaker, mass-produced and served up for guests, the poor and the rank-and-file monks. This weak beer was widely used as a milk substitute in the sixteenth century, when disease was rife in the growing towns and cities. So, by the Elizabethan age, beer was being used for both entertainment and medicinal purposes.

ELIZABETH I

While today drinking beer in the morning is unlikely and rare for most of us, in the sixteenth century the drink was championed as a health product. Not only did it contain only natural ingredients, but beer was a great source of vitamin B. So while modern man drinks beer for entertainment value, 400 years ago beer was viewed as a relaxant that contained antiseptic characteristics (weak beer barely had an alcohol content above two or three per cent). It is even said that Queen Elizabeth I drank a generous measure of ale every day at breakfast. History notes that she was also very particular about the beer that she drank and would often order in her own supplies of London-brewed ale whenever she went travelling around the country.

LAGER, LAGER, LAGER

You could say that lager was almost discovered by accident. In an attempt to store their beer out of the summer sun, German brewers stashed their beer-barrels in ice-packed caves and basements. They quickly discovered that the yeast behaved quite differently and that the fermentation process had been altered by the change of temperature. This 'cold fermentation' process continued to be pursued in central Europe, particularly in the German-speaking states where, in the 16th century, the Purity Pledge was passed, stating that only barley, malt, hops, yeast and water could be used in the production of beer. Naturally, this had nothing to do with the fact that the aristocracy had a monopoly on barley production...

SAMUEL WHITBREAD

Commercial brewing in Britain really took off in the eighteenth century, when pubs were drastically outnumbered by growing breweries. One of the early, pioneering brewers was Samuel Whitbread who started brewing pale ale at his brewery in Old Street in London in 1742. Whitbread's success was down to a new type of beer, the 'Porter', an unenticing mix of pale ale, traditional brown ale and stale beer (i.e. brew that had matured in its barrel for over a year). Named after the labourers in Manchester and Liverpool, the result was a strong, dark drink that had a caramel malt flavour and a fairly bitter aftertaste. (The Porter style of beermaking continued in popularity until the mid-1830s whereupon competition with mild ale and spirits – especially gin – caused its popularity to wane.)

By 1748, Whitbread had moved to bigger premises to concentrate on the production of his beer. With barely enough capital to get him started, he wisely invested in all of the latest mechanical technology (the steam engine, thermometer, mechanical mashers, etc.), choosing to store his porter-style brews in large vats or cisterns. Keeping the beer this way dramatically reduced the cost of producing it, and Whitbread quickly became rich by supplying his blended beverage to the local pubs and ale houses. If local, pub-based brewing hadn't died out by now, the rise of giant Porter beer tanks that could hold over 3,000 barrels of beer, certainly sounded its death knell. It is said that the famous German brewer, Gabriel Sedlmayer, later visited England in the 1830s to see Britain's brewing technology. He then returned to the continent to add the new techniques to German brewing, thus influencing the development of lager overseas. Of course, brewing on this 'industrial' scale wasn't without its problems. History records that a vat in London's Tottenham Court Road burst in the early 1800s, releasing a tidal wave of beer that demolished the brewery and drowned several people.

ARTHUR GUINNESS

While Samuel Whitbread was making a name for himself in London, an equally ambitious brewer, Arthur Guinness, was poised to embark on a famous career of his own. Come 1759, the businessman sold everything he owned and purchased an old and abandoned brewery in the centre of Dublin. Fortunately, a supply of unmalted barley was included in the brewery deal, but before Guinness could fully malt his stock ready for fermentation, a fire cruelly destroyed the majority of his stores. Without any money remaining to malt the barley, Guinness decided to use what remained of his un-malted barley to make up for the lack of the malted variety. To his surprise, the result was a dry stout, inky black, low in alcohol (about three per cent) and low in calories. The rest, of course, is history. Rich and smooth, the NHS once prescribed two eight-ounce helpings of Guinness to patients as an 'appetite stimulant, relaxant, mild laxative and sleep inducer'.